Canon
WORLD OF
PHOTOGRAPHY

Canon

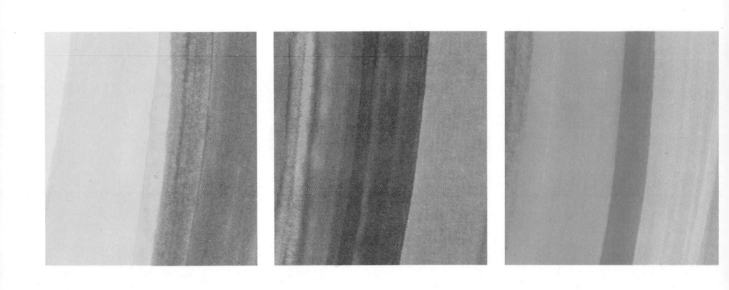

SLR Improver Course

Canon WORLD OF PHOTOGRAPHY

94 Crockford Boulevard
Scarborough, Ont.
M1R 3C5

© MCMLXXXIV Eaglemoss Limited, London
© MCMLXXXVI Jarrold Printing, Norwich

ISBN 0–921111–00–2 (set)
ISBN 0–921111–07–X

CONTENTS

INTRODUCTION

SLR Improver Course is a very special kind of book. It is an ideas book that has been compiled for photographers looking for ways of extending their hobby beyond basic snap shooting. It's a book that's packed full of hints and tips on different aspects of picture taking. It covers virtually every conceivable topic from lunar photography to landscapes.

Follow the chapters through and you will find the answer to all those nagging problems that have been spoiling your photographic image. Some of the information is pretty basic, but so are problems like red eye, over- and under-exposure and blurred pictures. Some of the techniques included, on the other hand, are quite advanced. So there is something here for everybody.

The Course is divided into many short sessions: Improving action photography; How to use selective focusing; Creative work with slides and negatives; What filters can do for your pictures, are just some of the topics covered. Each section is illustrated with descriptive photographs and diagrams and step by step sequences are included to clarify the more technical points.

Two thirds of the text deals with improving camera techniques and making the most of different lenses and camera accessories. The final section is all about processing films and making contact prints and enlargements. That's the stage you reach when the photography bug bites hard – which it has a habit of doing as you begin to improve your images and get hooked on picture taking.

Problem solving for better pictures

In photography there is nothing quite so disappointing as the picture which does not come out, or which fails completely to capture the interest or excitement of the subject which made you want to take the picture in the first place.

Can you honestly say that you have never made some of the mistakes illustrated here? Even the most experienced photographers occasionally take shots where the subject looks too small and gets lost, or where the exposure is completely wrong, or where the camera case appears in the picture. Even the very first stage of putting the film into the camera can be hazardous. Do you always remember to engage both sides of the perforations on the sprocket wheels and to watch the rewind knob as you wind on?

Avoiding these mistakes is only the first step to taking better pictures. You also need to learn what to look for in the viewfinder and to understand your camera.

CAMERA SHAKE
Problem: picture blurred overall.
Cause: moving the camera as you release the shutter, either through wrong technique or through not coping with difficult conditions such as shooting from a moving vehicle.
Solution: learn how to hold the camera correctly for steadiness, or use a tripod for support; which film to choose to ensure fast shutter speeds, and when to use flash.

POOR FOCUS
Problem: part or sometimes all of the picture blurred and fuzzy.
Cause: focusing incorrectly, or on the wrong part of the subject. The aperture chosen may not allow sharp focus throughout. The subject may be too close for focusing, or you may need some form of viewfinder eyepiece correction.
Solution: read chapter 3 to learn all about focusing.

SUBJECT MOVEMENT
Problem: subject blurred, streaked or double imaged but background sharp.
Cause: chosen shutter speed too slow to stop subject movement.
Solution: learn how the shutter works and how speeds can be chosen to stop action; how to capture action by panning; how to use viewpoint to minimize movement blur; how to push film to get fast speeds in poor light; how to anticipate peaks in the action, or use flash to stop it completely, or how to make subject blur work for you.

THINGS IN THE WAY
Problem: dark, blurred blobs or parts of the picture obscured.
Cause: things obstructing the lens – hair, case flaps, flash cables, fingertips; filters that are too small; lens hoods.
Solution: no current SLR shows you 100% of what the film sees, and with viewing at full aperture intrusions close to the lens can be too out of focus to be noticeable. This book explains how to use camera controls and accessories to ensure that you get only what you want in the picture.

GHOSTING AND FLARE
Problem: patches of spreading light, flares, or an overall weak, flat picture.
Cause: light entering the lens directly or at an angle and scattering.
Solution: learn how to use a lens hood; how to use your own hand as a lens shade, or to change the composition or camera angle, and how to use filters to make flare work for you.

OVER-EXPOSURE
Problem: picture too pale and washed out.
Cause: too much light allowed to reach the film. Aperture, shutter speed or film speed set wrongly; metering cell obstructed or misled by lighting conditions, or even faulty. Too fast a film loaded, or flash used too close to the subject. Lens failing to stop down correctly.
Solution: learn how to use an exposure meter, and learn the rules of thumb for exposures in typical conditions. Learn about choosing films, and camera checking.

UNDER-EXPOSURE
Problem: picture too dark, or print looks muddy with too little detail in shadows.
Cause: insufficient light reaching the film. Aperture, shutter speed or film speed set wrongly; meter fooled by frontal direct light. Film suffers reciprocity law failure, or flash fails.
Solution: as for over-exposure. Learn how to handle difficult lighting conditions. And how to push film to rescue mistakes.

CONTRASTY LIGHTING
Problem: ugly shadows with no detail, highlight areas washed out.
Cause: the human eye adapts rapidly to accommodate wide changes in brightness, but film does not.
Solution: follow this book to find out how to match the contrast range of the subject to the film; learn about fill-in reflectors, flash in sunlight; and how to compensate in the darkroom for excess contrast in the printing original.

FILLING THE FRAME
Problem: the subject looks tiny or insignificant, so the picture lacks impact.
Cause: you are too far away for the focal length of lens in use, you have tried to include too much, or you have framed the subject incorrectly.
Solution: the viewfinder is your picture frame and you have to look at the image, not through the camera. Look at the area of the picture taken up by the main subject compared to the total area.
● Bad positioning of the subject. Above, the photographer focused on the girl's face, which is correct, but then took the picture without re-framing to make better use of the height of the frame.

● Not getting close enough. The photographer has given as much prominence to the body and legs of his subject as to the face, but usually the face is the most expressive, interesting and individual feature. So this should be given most emphasis.
For the second picture our photographer corrected these errors, got closer and filled the frame. And you can see the difference in impact and interest which has resulted.

How to use your SLR viewfinder

The best possible way to see the shot you want to take with any camera is to look at the image formed by the lens – the picture which is focused on to the film. But to do this you would have to remove the film and the back of the camera, which is of course impractical.

The solution to this is the single lens reflex camera's viewfinder. The image from the lens is reflected by a 45° angled mirror on to the viewing screen (usually at 90° to the film) in the camera top.

Most SLR cameras have a pentaprism viewing system so that you can see the image through an eyepiece on the camera back.

The SLR is held at eye-level, the eyepiece magnifies the viewing screen, and the image seen is the right way up and the right way round. The magnified image assists you to see details and, with a 50mm lens, the scale is almost the same as that seen by the unaided eye.

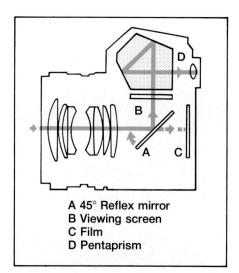

A 45° Reflex mirror
B Viewing screen
C Film
D Pentaprism

To allow accurate focusing the SLR focusing screen and the film are both the same distance from the lens. When the shutter release is pressed the 45° mirror (A) swings up and covers the screen (B). The shutter then uncovers, and therefore exposes, the film (C). Without a pentaprism (D) the image on the focusing screen would appear mirror-reversed from left to right (or upside down if the camera is used on its side for

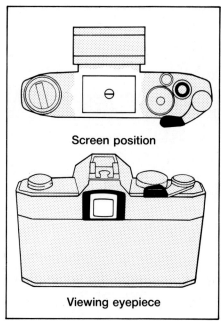

Screen position

Viewing eyepiece

vertical compositions). You would also have to look down into the camera to see the screen. The advantage of a pentaprism is that however you hold the camera, the image is the right way round.

USING THE FINDER SCREEN
SLR viewing screens are often bright and clear, and it is easy to forget to look at the composition after focusing on the subject. Don't forget to look at what is happening at the edges and corners, as well as at the centre of the frame. Merely being aware of the entire frame area can improve many compositions. A common mistake is to place the subject dead-centre in the frame.
The example above shows the effect of allowing a central focusing area to act as an aiming device – a bulls-eye composition. This is too easy to do, so try to ignore the central ring when finalizing the picture's composition after focusing.

When you concentrate solely on the centre of the viewfinder, parts of the subject at the frame edges can go unnoticed. It is difficult to cut off heads with an SLR camera, but it is easy to lose feet or hands unintentionally. This is common in portraits (with hands) and in groups (with feet). If there is danger of accidental cut-off, reposition your subject or move the camera to avoid the problem.

You must be equally careful that irrelevant details do not intrude into the frame edges. If something is in the background it may be acceptable, but a tiny part of an object or person showing near to or in front of the subject is distracting, like the out of focus red sleeve in the picture above. The simple solution is to make a final check on the frame edges before you release the shutter.

HORIZONTAL OR VERTICAL?

All SLR cameras are designed to handle best horizontally, rather than vertically. When you lift a camera to your eye the natural tendency is to use it in the most comfortable way. For the majority of photographers that tends to mean holding the camera horizontally between your hands to take horizontal pictures. But this does not suit every subject. In the photograph above, for example, the photographer has used only a thin slice of the available frame for what is a naturally vertical subject. It is particularly important to frame the subject carefully when shooting slides, as it is not easy to improve the composition later by cropping unwanted detail.

Get used to holding your camera like this for vertical compositions. Right-handed people usually find this grip more comfortable. You should be able to switch from a horizontal to a vertical grip without changing hands.

See how a vertical subject benefits from a vertical composition. The closer viewpoint gives more detail and impact. Mixing upright and horizontal shots makes a set of pictures more interesting too.

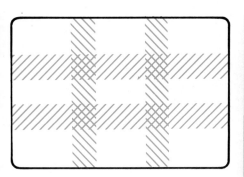

THE RULE OF THIRDS

Pictures somehow look much more interesting when the subject matter is well balanced in the frame. It is usually better to set the main subject to one side, or to place it at the top or bottom of the picture rather than dead-centre. The rule of thirds is a convenient guide to rapid, appealing composition in the viewfinder.
Put simply, the rule states that the zones about one-third in from the picture edges have the most visual attraction because that is where you naturally tend to look first. The visual impact of important subject details is highest at the points where the zones intersect (see diagram above).

If the horizon cuts the composition exactly in half, the photograph looks uneasy. Try to use the upper or lower one-third lines when deciding where to position the horizon.
If you are photographing a group of children the tallest one is best placed on

one of the vertical thirds rather than in the centre.
In the picture above the main elements, though simple, can be seen to coincide with the intersecting zones, making full use of the composition grid for a well balanced and pleasing photograph.

9

Focusing for sharper pictures

Lack of sharpness is a common picture fault. Often this is due to incorrect focusing. Pictures that look sharp when the negative or slide is examined often turn out to be unsharp when large prints are made or the slide is projected. Even worse, unimportant parts of the subject may be sharp while important parts are blurred.

For accurate focusing you must control the movement of the focusing ring precisely, know how to use focusing aids, what part of the subject to focus on, and how to recognize when something is in focus.

With standard lenses, small distances (a few millimetres on the focusing ring) represent large changes (several metres) in focusing distance, and therefore in the point of sharp focus.

Remember that the larger the size of print you are going to make, the more exact your focusing must be.

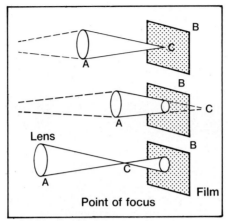

Point of focus

THE POINT OF FOCUS
A lens (A) focuses light rays into a cone shape. The rays converge to a sharp point (C), which is the point of sharp focus. If you put the film (B) at this point the image would be sharp. If the film is moved forwards or backwards, tiny discs of light are recorded on the film rather than sharply focused points. In practice the film does not move but the lens does in focusing. The image becomes progressively blurred the further you go from correct focus.

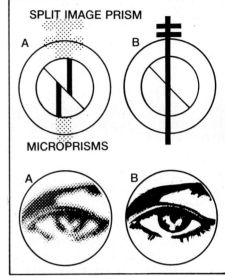

SPLIT IMAGE PRISM

MICROPRISMS

FOCUSING AIDS
Most focusing aids work by exaggerating incorrect focus. A split image prism produces two separate parts of the image (A) which only fit together when focus is correct (B). The circle of microprisms shimmers (A) until focus is correct (B).

WHERE TO FOCUS
Often the clearest part of the subject for focusing is not the focal point of the picture. Select the correct focusing area first, then try to find easy-to-focus detail within it.

The most common focusing errors occur in portraiture where the nose, teeth, or hair (above) are wrongly chosen as focusing points. It is the subject's eyes that hold the viewer's attention, and these or the eyelashes should always be the focusing target. After you have focused on the eyes, reposition the camera to give a pleasing composition.

In this portrait the eyes are perfectly sharp and the result is both appealing and captivating.

With more distant groups a striped shirt could be a good focusing target. Choose a sharp pattern, edge, line or strong texture, but whatever target you choose make sure it is stationary – a moving subject will not allow you enough time to focus.

Sight the subject and turn the focusing ring until the image in the viewfinder looks sharp. Turn the ring gently back and forth to double-check that the image you are focusing on can't be made to appear any sharper.

IS YOUR EYESIGHT GOOD ENOUGH?

It is possible that despite taking great pains to focus accurately, your pictures are still not pin sharp. Even if you do not need to wear spectacles all the time it could be that your eyesight is not good enough to judge the point of sharpest focus in the camera viewfinder.

When you look through the viewfinder of an SLR, you are in fact examining a small ground glass screen through a magnifying system. The eyepiece on the back of the camera viewfinder is a small magnifying glass focused on the viewing screen. It is designed for people with normal vision or slight short-sightedness. Long-sighted people can often focus at close distances (about 1 metre) and need spectacles only for close, detailed work. Short-sighted people cannot focus on distant subjects. Both groups can, however, normally focus on a subject between 1 and 2 metres away. Viewfinders are therefore set up to simulate this distance, but this may not work for you if you are extremely long- or short-sighted. Also mild astigmatism, another common sight defect, can make it impossible to see enough detail for precise focusing.

Checking eyesight: remove the lens and shine a domestic light bulb into the camera from about 1 metre away. If your eyesight is adequate the finely-grained surface of the screen should appear sharp.

Wearing spectacles: you should be able to see the whole screen when wearing spectacles for general use (not reading glasses). Fitting a rubber eye-cup to the eyepiece (above) makes viewing comfortable.

Contact lenses: focusing should be easy with contact lenses although the detail may not appear quite as fine. You may find it easier to focus with a split image prism rather than a microprism circle.

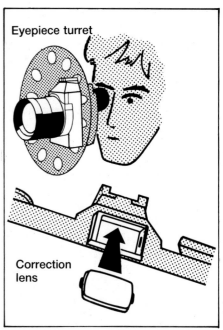

Eyepiece turret

Correction lens

CORRECTION LENSES

Long- or short-sight correction lenses can be fitted to most SLR eyepieces to remove the need for spectacles. An eyepiece turret shows correction needed.

USING YOUR FOCUSING RANGE

Most 50mm SLR lenses focus down to between 30cm and 60cm from the subject; 45cm is the most common limit. Although many of your pictures will be taken from more than 1 metre away, try to use the close-up range too for effective, detailed photographs.

Focusing accuracy is more critical the closer you are to the subject. At 45cm away, only 5 or 6cm depth in the subject will be sharp at medium apertures (around f8). How close you can afford to go depends on the depth of the subject and whether or not it is moving.

The picture above was taken over 1 metre away. The girls could move freely, and even if the kitten had moved it would have been in focus.

Moving in closer: in this shot, taken from about 60cm away, there is still leeway for small subject movement or a small focusing error.

The camera had to follow the subject all the time to keep it framed and focused correctly.

With this type of close shot it is easier to move the camera slightly backwards and forwards rather than to keep changing the focusing ring should the subject move.

To preserve your chosen composition keep the focusing distance constant rather than changing the setting on the focusing ring.

The whiskers of the kitten make a good test for focusing accuracy in this particular picture.

Minimum focusing distance: for this shot the camera was set on its minimum 30cm focusing distance and the camera was moved to and fro until focus on the kitten became sharp. By now even a sudden move back by the kitten would produce a blur. Note how the girl's hands are blurred. For shots like this you must view the focusing screen critically and learn to react quickly. With SLRs there is little risk of accidentally taking a picture closer than the minimum focusing distance allows because you can clearly see through the viewfinder that the image is blurred.

Always decide on the main subject first, frame up a rough composition, focus carefully, then finalize composition. There is no remedy for unsharp pictures.

How the aperture affects focus

The aperture has two main functions: to control how much light reaches the film in order to produce the correct exposure, and to control how much of the picture is in sharp focus.

Here we explore how the aperture affects depth of field, and how to choose the right f stop to create a picture that is easily sharply focused throughout or only sharp in parts.

Inside the SLR lens is a diaphragm made up of a circle of overlapping blades which produce a central round hole of variable diameter. This hole is called the aperture, and its size is given in f stops. By aperture, we mean effective aperture: that is, the diameter of the beam of light allowed to pass through. This can change according to where the diaphragm is inside the lens. The actual diameter of the diaphragm is of interest only to lens designers.

You cannot measure the true diameter of your lens aperture because it is behind at least one glass element, which distorts the size.

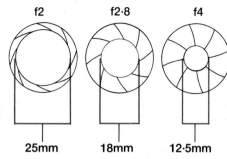

THE APERTURE SCALE
Your standard lens probably has at least seven apertures marked on its scale. These are drawn from the accepted series which progresses from f1 to f1·4, f2, f2·8, f4, f5·6, f8, f11, f16, f22, f32, and so on. Each number is one full f stop from each of the numbers next to it. Manufacturers like to have the largest possible maximum apertures on their lenses so the maximum value often does not coincide with an f stop from the scale. Values like f1·7 and f1·8 are common, and the lens shown here starts at f3·5. The step from the maximum aperture to the first f stop in the standard series is often less than one full stop. (In the case shown, f3·5 to f4 is a difference of only 1/3 stop.) Most aperture rings click-stop at each full f stop setting.

HOW f STOPS WORK
The f number describes the size of the aperture formed by the diaphragm blades in the lens. The number represents the focal length of the lens divided by the diameter of the aperture, so a 50mm lens with an aperture diameter of 25mm (50 ÷ 25) has an aperture value of f2.
However, the amount of light the aperture lets through depends on the area of the hole, not simply the diameter. If we halve the area of the f2 aperture, the diameter is 18mm and the aperture 2·8: f2·8 lets through half as much light as f2.
Each full f stop along the scale doubles or halves the amount of light allowed through. The larger the f number, the smaller the aperture.

SMALL APERTURES
Small apertures such as f11, f16 and f22 give progressively greater depth of field. They are useful for recording scenic shots of landscapes, city views and buildings, when you want both the foreground and the background to be as sharply focused as possible.
With shots of moving subjects a small aperture provides enough depth of field to minimize the effect of slight focusing errors. Small apertures are especially useful with close-ups since depth of field diminishes with decreasing camera-to-subject distances.

WIDE APERTURES
Wide apertures such as f2, f2·8 and f4 give shallow depth of field. This means that only objects just in front of or just behind the point on which you have focused are sharp. Objects closer to the lens or further away will be out of focus and therefore unsharp. Careful focusing is therefore critical. A wide aperture is useful for subjects like portraits and wildlife shots, as it helps to separate the subject from a potentially confusing background.
Wide apertures can also be used to lose intruding objects close to the lens such as wire netting.

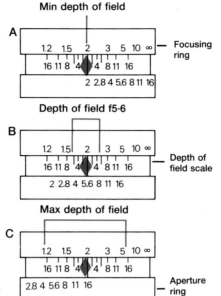

Min depth of field

A
1.2 1.5 2 3 5 10 ∞ — Focusing ring
16 11 8 4 4 8 11 16
2 2.8 4 5.6 8 11 16

Depth of field f5·6

B
1.2 1.5 2 3 5 10 ∞
16 11 8 4 4 8 11 16 — Depth of field scale
2 2.8 4 5.6 8 11 16

Max depth of field

C
1.2 1.5 2 3 5 10 ∞
16 11 8 4 4 8 11 16
2.8 4 5.6 8 11 16 — Aperture ring

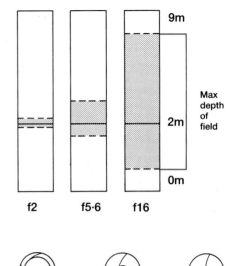

9m

2m — Max depth of field

0m

f2   f5·6   f16

A   B   C

DEPTH OF FIELD

The human eye appears to see everything in sharp focus, but the camera lens is more selective. The lens can create a picture which is sharp virtually throughout, or limit sharpness to only part of the scene. Depth of field describes the extent of the scene which is sharp in front of and behind the point on which you have focused. Depth of field is controlled mainly by aperture size – small apertures give more depth of field; large apertures give less.

As you can see from the picture above, focusing on one flower and using a large aperture puts the flowers closer to the camera and farther away out of focus. As a rule of thumb, ⅔ of the depth of field will be behind the point of focus and ⅓ in front.

DEPTH OF FIELD SCALE

The depth of field scale on the lens indicates how much of the scene will be sharp at a given aperture.

In the diagram above the f stops are marked on the aperture ring of the lens. Some of these numbers are repeated on the depth of field scale. With the lens set at f16 and focused on 2 metres the two 16s on the depth of field scale lie

opposite 1·2 metres and the equivalent of 8 metres on the focusing ring. This means that the part of the scene between 1·2 and 8 metres away from the camera is in focus, even though the lens is focused on one specific point. Therefore depth of field is 6·8 metres with these settings. Compare this with the much narrower depth of field for f5·6 and f2, shown in the diagram above.

USING THE VIEWFINDER

Most modern SLRs are equipped with fully automatic diaphragms so the screen image is always viewed at maximum aperture. This makes for easy focusing. Once an exposure has been made at working aperture, the diaphragm fully opens once again to give maximum screen brightness.

But beware! The wide aperture also means that only part of the scene in the viewfinder will be in focus. At the correct aperture for the shot the picture may be spoiled by something obscuring the lens or a distraction in the background which you had not noticed.

BACKGROUND INTRUSION

Small apertures such as f11 or f16 bring more of the picture depth into focus, but sometimes this can also be a disadvantage.

The sharp background may conflict with the subject as in the picture above, or accidental intrusions just in front of the lens that were invisible at maximum aperture may come into focus.

To avoid these problems, choose an aperture wide enough to limit the depth of sharp focus. Or if you have a depth of field preview button, use it to check the effect of stopping down before you take the picture.

DEPTH OF FIELD PREVIEW

Some SLRs have a depth of field preview button (arrowed). When pressed, this temporarily closes the lens diaphragm to the working aperture so you can check image sharpness through the viewfinder before taking the picture. The screen darkens, but usually you can still assess the effect.

Some lenses have a manual diaphragm, where turning the aperture ring actually closes or opens the blades. This means you have to preview the depth of field as the lens sees it. Compose and focus at maximum aperture then stop down to take the shot.

Shutter speeds and image sharpness

There are basically two types of camera shutter – the blade or leaf shutter and the focal plane shutter.

Blade or leaf shutters are located close to the lens. They are mostly associated with large and medium formats, as well as with non-reflex cameras. Focal plane shutters are the type used in most 35mm SLRs.

The main job of the shutter is simple. When it is closed it keeps out light. When the shutter release button is pressed the shutter opens and exposes the film to light. The longer it remains open, the more light reaches the film.

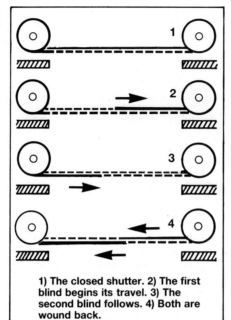

1) The closed shutter. 2) The first blind begins its travel. 3) The second blind follows. 4) Both are wound back.

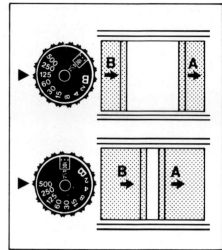

HOW THE SHUTTER WORKS
Most focal plane shutters consist of two blinds or curtains. These are usually made of special light-proof black cloth. The cloth type run horizontally across the film plane from left to right. When the shutter release button is pressed the first blind begins its travel, uncovering the film and exposing it to light. To end the exposure the second blind quickly follows the first and completely covers the film. When you

wind on, both blinds are pulled back across the film to their original position – all the time overlapping to keep out light. At the same time the springs are tensioned ready to propel the blinds forward when the shutter release button is pressed for the next exposure.

SHUTTER SPEEDS
The width of the gap between the two blinds is programmed by the shutter speed you choose. The slower the shutter speed, the later the second blind will follow the first and, therefore, the wider the gap between them. The diaphragm above shows the width of the gap when the shutter speed dial is set at 1/125 (top) and the difference in width when the shutter speed is set at 1/500 (bottom).

Hold the camera at eye-level

Pull gently upwards

STANCE
If you are not properly balanced while taking a picture you are likely to move the camera during the exposure, this will be most noticeable at slow shutter speeds.
Imagine yourself as a human tripod. Find some level ground and stand firmly with your legs slightly apart. For extra support you can lean against a tree or a wall, holding the camera against the upright surface.

HOLDING THE CAMERA
It is also important to hold the camera as steady as possible. Support it in the palm of your left hand, leaving your fingers free for focusing. This helps to prevent downward movement when you release the shutter. Your right hand should grip the side of the camera while your index finger releases the shutter. Remember: always keep your elbows tucked in – it is much easier to keep your hands steady if your arms are still.

USE A CAMERA BRACE
Another way to steady the camera is by continued upward tension. All you need is a length of light chain or non-stretch cord attached to the camera tripod screw with a spare tripod bush. The brace should be long enough to allow the camera to be held comfortably at eye-level with a loop or a short length secured under your foot. To steady the camera pull gently upwards until the brace becomes taut.

14

Squeeze the shutter release gently

CAMERA SHAKE
Using a shutter speed slower than 1/60 of a second when hand-holding the camera increases the chances of your picture suffering from camera shake. No matter how steady your hands, it is almost impossible to prevent some movement. The act of pressing the shutter release button is likely to create slight downward movement, while both the swing of the mirror and the travel of the shutter blinds can cause vibration. The result will ultimately be loss of sharpness in your picture.

TEST YOURSELF
If you really don't believe that your hands shake while holding the camera, try this simple experiment. Go outside one evening, after the street lamps have gone on, and take pictures of some of them. Use different shutter speeds, preferably throughout the range. At slower speeds the light from the lamps will faithfully trace out any camera movement (above left). The results will show at what speeds it is safe for you to hand-hold the camera without getting camera shake.

RELEASING THE SHUTTER
There is only one way to operate the shutter release button correctly, and that is to squeeze slowly. If you jab at it the camera will move. Rest your finger on the button and, slowly and gently, squeeze down on it almost as if you were pressing the trigger of a gun. Keep your finger pressed down until the exposure is complete.
You may find that it helps to breathe out just before pressing the shutter release button, and relax while taking the picture.

CARRY A BEAN BAG
A bean bag is a useful accessory for steadying the camera. It can be placed on almost any support and pushed into the right shape for the camera. This means that you can rest the camera on railings, cars or tree trunks without risk of damage. Bean bags are easy to make or can be bought cheaply. They are also easy to carry about with you. If you don't have one, you can use a rolled up jumper or towel as a substitute in an emergency.

WHY BE SO CAREFUL?
The size of the picture above is about average for a normal print, and yet it is about 12 times bigger than a 35mm slide or negative. This means that any slight degree of blur, which you may not even see on a 35mm slide but which the film will have faithfully recorded, will be 12 times more noticeable on a print this size. Even worse, if you project a slide the image may be 120 times bigger – and so will the mistakes. So it is worth taking the extra trouble to ensure your pictures are sharp.

15

Shutter speeds and moving subjects

The main function of the shutter is to control the amount of time that the film is exposed to light.

If the subject being photographed moves while the shutter is open, blur will be recorded on the film. The amount of blur will depend on three things – how fast the subject is moving, the direction it is moving in and how long the shutter remains open.

Most cameras have a range of shutter speeds from 1 second to 1/1000 second. To eliminate movement, or to freeze the subject in mid-motion, you must use a fast shutter speed. For most moving subjects shutter speeds over 1/250 are needed to freeze action.

Usually you will want to freeze action completely. Other times you may prefer to have some streaks or blur just to show how fast something in the picture is moving. The choice is yours.

A SLOW SPEED
When lighting conditions are poor you will have to use a slow shutter speed. You cannot then stop subject movement and so must either accept blur or use a static subject. The shutter speed used here was ⅛.

A FAST SPEED
To stop subject movement you will have to use a fast shutter speed. Just how fast will depend on the speed of subject movement in relation to camera position (see table). For this shot the shutter speed was 1/1000.

PANNING
If you use a slower shutter speed you can still get a sharp picture of a moving subject by following the movement with the camera while pressing the shutter release button. This is known as panning and is often used in sports photography.

By moving the camera so that the subject is kept in the same place in the viewfinder all the time the shutter is open you will get good subject sharpness. The background, however, will record as blurred, giving a strong impression of speed.

HOW TO PAN
Stand firmly, and pre-focus on the spot where you plan to take the picture. Turn towards the oncoming subject and follow it. Press the shutter release, but keep following the subject until after the end of the exposure.

SPEED AND MOVEMENT

The exact effect of subject movement depends on how far the camera is from the subject and the direction in which the subject is travelling.

The pictures above were all taken at a shutter speed of 1/30. The degree of blur is much more pronounced when subject movement is directly across the camera (right) than when the movement is head on (left). When subject movement is at 45° to the camera (centre) the amount of blur recorded is somewhere between the two.

Use the simple table shown here as a guide to the shutter speeds required to get a sharp picture of moving subjects.

Subject at	Pedestrian (5km/h)	Runner (15km/h)	Cyclist (25km/h)	Horses (40km/h)	Traffic (65km/h)	Train (120km/h)
1m	1/1000					
3m	1/500	1/1000				
5m	1/250	1/500	1/1000			
10m	1/125	1/250	1/500	1/1000		
30m	1/60	1/125	1/250	1/500	1/1000	1/2000

The shutter speeds given above are for subjects moving directly across the picture area.

For subjects that are moving at an angle of 45° to the camera you can use the next slowest shutter speed and still get a sharp picture.

If the subject is moving directly away from or towards the camera two speeds slower than the shutter speed given above can be used.

When panning, try experimenting with shutter speeds faster than 1/30 of a second.

  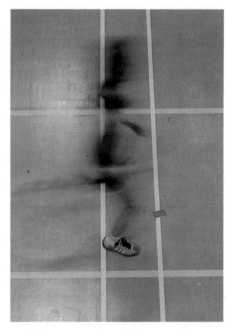

SHARP. . .

The camera is unique in its ability to freeze movement, and provides an unequalled opportunity to study precise detail in a moving subject.

The shutter speed used for the picture above was 1/1000.

. . .OR BLURRED?

Pin-sharp motion shots can look very dramatic but they may also appear to be rather artificial.

In this picture the slower shutter speed of 1/8 gives a greater sense of the flow of rushing water.

CREATIVE BLUR

When a slow speed is used a moving subject can be so blurred it almost disappears, while motionless parts record as usual.

This photograph of an athlete's foot was taken at 1/8.

17

Getting to grips with exposure

The exposure controls on an SLR camera are the aperture ring and the shutter speed dial. Together they work to control the amount of light which reaches the film.

When light reaches the film it affects the light sensitive silver salts in the emulsion coating. Light coming from the brightest areas in the subject has greatest impact. The effect is made visible by developing the film in suitable chemicals. The resultant negative has images reversed in tone. Printing the negative creates a positive picture.

To get the correct exposure – that is, a final picture which shows a full range of tones – the film must receive the right amount of light. Too little exposure to light will produce a thin negative and so a dark print; too much exposure will produce a dense negative and the final image produced on the print will be too light.

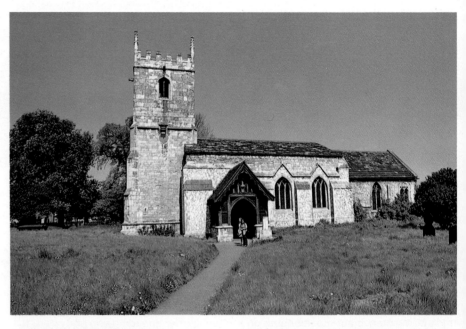

CORRECT EXPOSURE
In a print from a correctly exposed negative, the darkest shadow areas of the subject reproduce as a full black, and the lightest highlights as white, with a full range of tones between.

The picture above is correctly exposed. The highlight areas in the walls of the church print as clear white. The darkest shadow areas, are solid black. The roof, trees, grass and flowers clearly show a range of tones and shades of colour.

CONTROLLING EXPOSURE
As already mentioned, to control the exposure you must control the amount of light falling on the film. There are two ways of doing this. The first is to vary the size of the aperture, and so control the intensity of the light passing through the lens. The second is to alter the shutter speed setting and so control the length of time for which light falls on the film emulsion. A combination of these two controls determines the amount of exposure.
You can get the same exposure from a range of aperture and shutter speed combinations. These diagrams show that a wide aperture used in conjunction with a fast shutter speed (f2·8 + 1/1000) will give the same amount of light, and so the same exposure, as a small aperture and a slow shutter speed (f11 + 1/60). With an aperture of f5·6 a shutter speed of 1/250 will also give the same exposure. The yellow panels on the far right all represent the same exposure from the same subject. The left-hand column represents the intensity of light passing through the lens at various aperture sizes and the middle column shows light allowed through at various shutter speed settings.

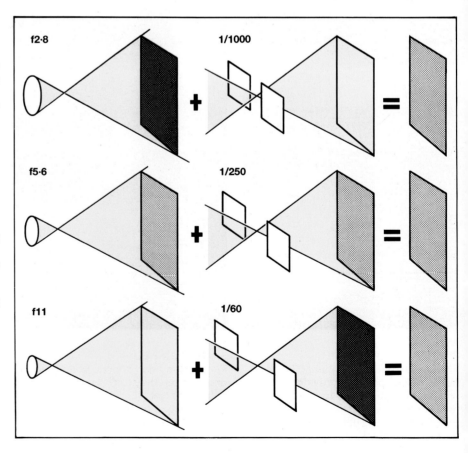

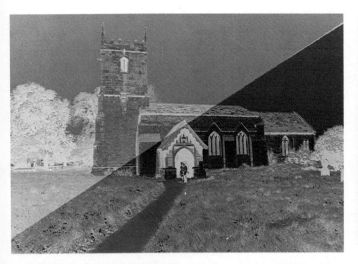

BADLY EXPOSED NEGATIVES

A negative can be incorrectly exposed in two ways. If too much light reaches the film, the emulsion turns too black and the negative is over-exposed. If too little light falls on the film not enough of the emulsion is turned black and the negative is under-exposed. An under-exposed negative (top left half, above) looks thin and washed out. There are clear areas where parts of the dark subject have not been recorded. An over-exposed negative (bottom right half) looks thick or dense and blocked up. The light areas of the subject may be so dense on the negative that detail is lost.

PRINTS FROM BADLY EXPOSED NEGATIVES

Given the same printing exposure, a thin, under-exposed negative will give a very dark print, while a thick, over-exposed one will give a thin, light print. Changing the printing exposure to compensate can improve the results, but you can't put back detail which has not been recorded on the original negative. For example, the top left half of the picture, from the under-exposed negative, lacks detail in the shadow areas of the church, and the mid-tones are hard to distinguish. The bottom right half, from the over-exposed negative, is washed out, and the light areas are lacking in detail.

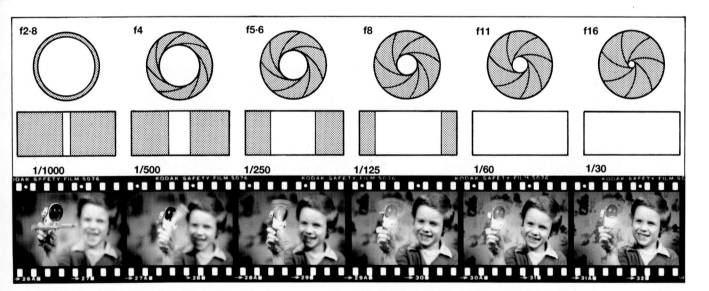

COMBINING SHUTTER AND APERTURE

For most lighting conditions there is a range of shutter speed and aperture combinations which will give correct exposures. What you have to remember is that if you close down the aperture by one stop you halve the amount of light that it lets through. To obtain the correct exposure at this smaller aperture you must therefore use the next slowest shutter speed to double the time for which the film is exposed to light, and so compensate for the loss of intensity. The diagrams above show six combinations which all give the same exposure.

ONE EXPOSURE, SEVERAL CHOICES

Although it is possible to get the same exposure using a number of different combinations, as the strip of pictures above illustrates, the effect on depth of field and movement will vary.

The combination that you choose for a particular subject will depend on the effect you want to produce. If you want to freeze fast movement you must set a fast shutter speed first and then adjust the aperture to provide the correct exposure. If you want to control depth of field set the aperture first and then adjust the shutter speed for the correct exposure.

Using your camera's exposure meter

Almost all modern SLRs have an exposure meter built into them. These meters are battery powered and use one or two light-sensitive cells to measure the amount of light coming through the lens.

These TTL meters are easy to use because they are coupled to the camera's shutter speed dial and aperture ring.

TTL meters come in two different types, stop-down and full aperture. Stop-down meters measure the light with the lens closed down to the taking aperture set on the lens. Full aperture meters measure at the maximum aperture of the lens but (as long as the lens has the correct linkages with the camera body) make an allowance to compensate for the smaller aperture actually set. Stopping the lens down darkens the viewfinder, so full aperture metering is better.

Some cameras have special spot-metering systems which measure exposure from a small, selected area of the subject.

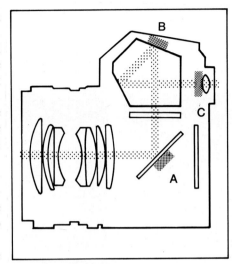

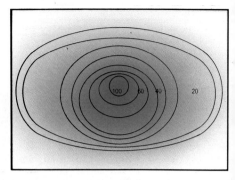

METERING CELLS
The metering cell or cells may be sited in one of three main positions in order to measure the light on its path from the lens to your eye (see dotted band in diagram). These are (A) on or behind the surface of the mirror, (B) in the top of the prism, or (C) next to the viewfinder eyepice. The positioning governs the weighting of the light reading, and also the extent to which the meter can be misled by light entering through the viewfinder eyepiece.

SENSITIVITY
A TTL meter can measure all the light coming through the lens and give an average reading, or measure the central spot where the subject is most likely to be placed. Average metering works well with average scenes. Spot metering works best for difficult subjects.

Most TTL meters measure all or most of the picture area but take most notice of the centre of the frame. This gives centre-weighted metering, which is illustrated in the diagram: the strength of the colour shows the degree of meter sensitivity. As the top of the picture often contains sky, many cameras have meters where the main area of sensitivity is below the centre, or centre-bottom weighting.

HOW WEIGHTING WORKS
Most pictures are taken with the camera held horizontally, with the subject placed in the centre of the frame, towards the bottom. The main subject is what you want to be correctly exposed, so it makes sense to have the TTL meter pay most attention to this area when measuring exposure. The result is a centre-bottom weighted metering pattern. It works perfectly with average subjects, such as the house in the picture above, where the main area of subject interest coincides with the metering pattern.

WHERE WEIGHTING FAILS
Weighting fails when the meter's area of sensitivity does not correspond exactly to the subject, as in the picture above. The same house has been photographed in the same lighting, so logically the exposure should be the same. But with the camera turned for a vertical shot, part of the sensitive centre-bottom area is reading a patch of sky. It has responded to the extra brightness by closing down the aperture, thus under-exposing the main subject. In such cases, it is best to take a meter reading with the camera horizontal first.

DIFFICULT SUBJECTS
A TTL meter is calibrated to give correct exposure for a mid grey tone. This works with coloured subjects containing a wide range of tones because if you mix them all together the result is, on average, a mid grey tone.

However, where a subject is divided into clearly separated dark and light areas, this may not be so. In the picture above, the meter has given an average reading for the bright subject in the centre and the dark surround. The result is that the centre is over-exposed and the surrounding arch under-exposed.

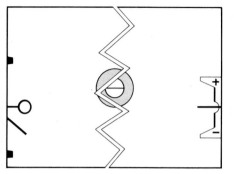
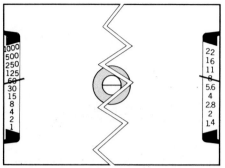
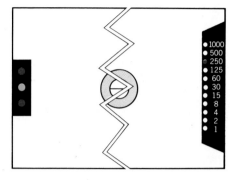

VIEWFINDER DISPLAYS
There are many types of display to show the meter reading in the viewfinder. Moving needle displays are common.
Match needle systems (above left): the meter needle swings up and down according to the amount of light being measured. You adjust the speed or aperture until a second needle (usually with an 'O' end to assist alignment) is positioned over it for correct exposure.
Centre needle systems (above right): the needle swings up and down as before. You adjust shutter speed or aperture to centre the needle between two marks to obtain correct exposure. With displays like the two above, there is usually no indication of the actual values of shutter and aperture set.

SCALE READINGS
A refinement of the match-needle system is to have the needle move over either a shutter speed scale or an aperture scale on one side of the viewfinder. The other value (either the aperture or the speed) may be shown elsewhere in the finder.
Aperture priority (above left): with the aperture set, the needle points to the speed required for correct exposure.
Shutter priority (above right): with the speed set, the needle points to the aperture required for correct exposure. In each case, the photographer sets one of the exposure values manually. With auto-exposure SLRs, however, this is performed automatically: such cameras may be shutter or aperture priority.

LED DISPLAYS
Needle displays are delicate and prone to mechanical failure, especially if cameras are dropped. Many electronic cameras now use LEDs (light emitting diodes) instead of needles, but in practice these are used in the same way.
Centering systems (above left): simple LED systems work just like centre needle ones. Usually two red LEDs are used to show under- or over-exposure, and a central green LED lights up for correct exposure.
Scale systems (above right): use an LED for each shutter speed, and work just like aperture priority systems: the LED next to the correct speed lights up. LEDs are less prone to mechanical failure and are easier to see in the dark.

SELECTIVE METERING
In this problem picture, the choice was between (1) giving correct exposure for the surrounding arch, allowing the centre of the frame to be over-exposed; and (2) giving correct exposure for the central subject, letting the archway be under-exposed. For the picture above, the second alternative was chosen. Whichever the choice, the method is to use the camera to take a meter reading from the main subject only, setting or holding that exposure, then returning to the original composition to take the shot. This is called selective metering.

BACKLIGHTING
The most common situation requiring selective metering is when taking portraits with the subject positioned against the light, or against a bright area such as a patch of sky. The meter has no way of knowing what the main subject is, and sets the exposure to take into account the bright background. It therefore sets either too fast a shutter speed or too small an aperture. The result is shown in the picture above – the subject's face comes out under-exposed – too dark in the picture. There are three ways to correct this problem.

BACKLIGHT CONTROL
To get correct exposure, (1) if you have a spot meter, use it to take a reading from the face only. (2) With an averaging meter, go up to the subject and take a close up reading from the face. (3) Take the reading normally but override the meter by opening up an extra 1½ to 2 stops to compensate for the backlighting. Many automatic SLRs have overrides for this purpose: you simply set × 2 on an exposure compensation (EV) dial. Some automatic SLRs gave a push-button backlight control which gives 1½ stops extra automatically.

How to handle exposure problems

When you have been using a TTL or hand-held meter for some time you will find you can often predict the correct exposure simply by looking at the scene you want to photograph.

There are advantages in being able to predict the correct exposure. The first is that if by some chance your meter is giving inaccurate readings (perhaps the battery is run down) you will be able to tell. If on a sunny day, for instance, your meter tells you the correct exposure is f4 at 1/60 you can be fairly sure that something is wrong – either the ISO speed is set wrongly, or the meter is faulty, or the subject is in very unusual lighting. In any case, you must make some correction.

Often you can look at the weather and say, 'This is a 1/250 at f5·6 day, with ISO 100 film' and be right. Of course, light variations and unusual subjects may need alterations but you can learn very quickly.

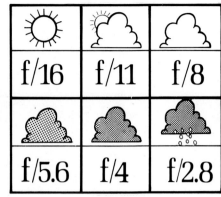

SAFE EXPOSURE SETTING
Simple cartridge cameras often have only one setting but still produce good results on bright days. A manual SLR can be set in the same way to give exactly the same chance of usable exposures. This can be useful when you need to shoot very quickly.
Just set the camera at 1/250 at f8 if using medium speed film, or 1/500 at f11 for fast film. This safe setting is most suitable for use with negative films for prints (slides need more accurate exposure). The success rate for this with simple photographs is higher than you might expect.

ESTIMATING EXPOSURE
You can use the above table for estimating exposure with any make of film, as long as you know the ISO speed. Set the shutter speed to the nearest setting, numerically, to the ISO film speed. For an ISO 400 film use 1/500, for ISO 100 use 1/125, for ISO 64 use 1/60. Now just read off the aperture underneath the appropriate weather symbol. Open up by one extra f stop in winter, one extra 1-2 hours from sunset or sunrise, and one extra for dark subjects or close-ups (add the extra f stops together for these in combination).

DEALING WITH DARK BACKGROUNDS
If the greater part of the picture is dark, but the camera's meter reads from the whole scene, it will try to give too much exposure to compensate for the lack of light in the background. Unless you want this dark area to record lighter you have to adjust the indicated exposure by cutting it down, giving one or two stops less exposure or by using a faster shutter speed. The picture will then have a rich, dark background on which a correctly exposed subject stands out, rather than a grey, washed out background with a burned-out detail-free subject. On cameras with exposure compensation, dial – 1.

DEALING WITH LIGHT BACKGROUNDS
If you have a fairly dark subject against a much brighter background the reverse happens: the meter receives too much light and indicates less exposure than is needed, resulting in a picture with a grey background and a very dark subject with no detail. So, you should increase your exposure, much as you would for back-lit subjects. You can do this by using a backlight control button, an exposure over-ride dial set to + 1, or by taking a close-up reading from the subject. If the two scenes above had been lit the same, the exposure needed would have been the same. The meter reading, however, would have shown at least two stops difference.

22

BRACKETING

Once you get to know the kind of exposures to expect there will be times when the meter reading seems to disagree with common sense. This happens most often in difficult light and you may then find you have to rely on guesswork.

Bracketing is the simplest solution to any doubts about exposure accuracy. As in the strip above, you take a number of shots instead of one. The correct exposure might be one stop more or less than the indicated exposure. By making three exposures, including one at one stop more and one at one stop less than the meter reading, you can be fairly sure of a usable result. If in real doubt, you can make more exposures, or even bracket at half-stop intervals.

LATITUDE

Look again at the strip above and you will see that the central three exposures are all fairly good. In fact, detail is visible in all five of them, although the densest shot received only 1/16th of the exposure of the lightest one. The film can thus cope with a reasonable amount of exposure error, and the ability to do this is called latitude. With films for prints, variations in exposure of one stop either side of the right setting can be corrected undetectably during printing. The strip above was taken on colour slide film, where there is no chance to correct exposure afterwards, but the central three slides are all usable. So, bracketing and natural film latitude make estimating exposure a better risk than you might otherwise expect.

FILM ECONOMY

If you took a strip of five exposures for each subject you would be wasting film. By using experience and common sense, you should be able to guard against exposure error by taking a maximum of one additional shot. Only bracket if the subject is unrepeatable, vitally important, or if you think the meter reading is inaccurate.

With slide films bracket at half-stop intervals. With print films, bracket at full stop intervals. For extra economy, in general with slide films, bracket only on the side of under-exposure, and with print films only on the side of over-exposure, as this ensures detail is retained as far as possible. Unless the lighting conditions are very difficult, one of the exposures should be correct.

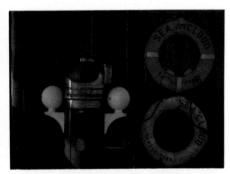

DELIBERATE OVER-EXPOSURE

If the subject is predominantly light and not too contrasty it may benefit from a light and delicate rendering. Try giving two or even three stops of deliberate over-exposure. This will soften the colours and produce a soft, atmospheric picture. Results are best when the important detail of the subject is in the mid-tones and darker parts of the picture. The lighter areas are certain to lose detail.

Suitable subjects include snow scenes, where the TTL meter reading will expose to give snow grey tones instead of whites, and make landscapes bathed in early morning mist look like the picture above.

DELIBERATE UNDER-EXPOSURE

Subjects in bright light can often benefit from a half or whole stop under-exposure. This increases the saturation of the colours and produces a richer, more dramatic picture. It also gives solid, black shadows, so if you want to retain important detail in shadow areas this technique is obviously unsuitable. It works best with strongly lit, textured, solid subjects with definite highlight areas containing important detail.

The picture above was underexposed by one stop to ensure maximum colour saturation. Under-exposure loses details in shadow areas but improves the highlights.

TIME EXPOSURES

The B setting on your camera's shutter speed dial holds the shutter open and allows you to give exposures of longer than one second. This is particularly useful in low lighting conditions.

Often these long exposures are beyond the range of the meter on your camera so you will have to experiment to get acceptable results. Bracket each shot, and as a rule of thumb start by giving a longer exposure than you think you would need. For sharp pictures you must use a tripod or other support, but movement blur can also be exciting. The picture of car headlights above was taken from another car during an exposure of 2 seconds at f5·6.

Choosing the right film

There may seem to be a bewildering range of films on offer, but once you have chosen a brand, there are only three main types: colour negative, colour slide and black and white negative. Each has its own characteristics and the choice of a particular type or film speed depends on personal preference, the subject to be photographed and the lighting.

COLOUR NEGATIVE
This film is used to produce colour prints. The cost of the film does not include processing, and there is a wide choice of process-and-print services available. Once the film is exposed you can return it to the dealer for developing and printing, send it away to a mail order process-and-print firm, or you can take it to a professional colour laboratory directly.

Alternatively, if you have the facilities you can process the film yourself. Prints are made from the negative (above left) after the film has been developed.
Prints from 35mm colour negatives are normally 85 × 125mm (enprint size) but the professional labs do offer larger sizes, such as 180 × 125mm, and 200 × 150mm prints at higher cost.

COLOUR SLIDE (REVERSAL)
This film is for direct production of positive colour transparencies (above centre) for projection.
Some slide films include processing in their price, such as Fujichrome and Kodachrome.
Others (Ektachrome, Fujichrome Professional, Barfen CR100 and Agfachrome) do not and must be returned to the dealer or a laboratory for paid processing.
According to the number of pictures you wish to take, you can choose from rolls of either 20 or 36 exposures.
If you want copies of your colour slides you can have duplicates or even prints made. However, these are likely to be of poorer quality than the original and fairly expensive.

BLACK AND WHITE NEGATIVE
This is the film used to produce black and white prints. The price of the film does not include processing.
The chemicals and simple equipment required for processing black and white negative film are inexpensive and readily available from photographic dealers, so most photographers who regularly use black and white negative film tend to do their own processing and make all their own prints.
Good results are not difficult to achieve, and this has led to a decline in commercial black and white processing, which is now often more expensive than colour. An example of a black and white negative is shown above right (most monochrome 35mm films have a tinted base, usually blue-grey).

FILM SPEEDS
Film speeds reflect the degree of the film's sensitivity to light and are usually marked in ISO numbers of between 25 and 1600. Each speed is appropriate for a different lighting condition.
The meter on your camera is linked to the film speed dial (above). Therefore, it is important that you set the right film speed before you begin to expose the film. When you have loaded a film in the camera, turn the film speed dial until the marker corresponds to the ISO number of the film you are using. The meter will then give correct readings.

If your camera is brand new, you may well be saved the chore of setting the film speed altogether. For some time now, film makers have been putting speed information and other sensitivity data on every film cassette. Known as DX coding, Kodak developed the original system and other film manufacturers are now using it too. The code looks rather like a draughtboard in miniature. It can be picked up and acted on by a DX-reading camera, so removing yet another possible error at the film loading stage. As far as cameras of the future are concerned, the potential is there for DX coding to tell the camera not only the film speed, but also the number of exposures on the roll and even how much the pictures can be over- or under-exposed without loss of quality.

MEDIUM SPEED FILMS
Medium speed films (ISO 80 to 200) are intended for all types of photography. They are sensitive enough to light to be used on dull days, with small flash guns, and can be used without a tripod in most conditions.

PROS AND CONS
Medium speed films can cope with a great range of subjects and conditions, give good colour, fairly fine grain and have a good latitude to exposure error. They are really only inadequate in extreme lighting conditions.

SLOW FILMS

Slow films, starting at around ISO 25, are the least sensitive to light, requiring wider apertures or longer shutter speeds to give more exposure. On very dulll days or in dim light (dusk, interiors etc) the use of a tripod may be necessary. A typical exposure in bright sunlight with an ISO 25 film, the slowest normally used, is 1/125 at f8. With slow films you also have to use wider apertures for flash or restrict flash to close distances. The slowest colour slide film is Kodachrome 25. Following that in speed, there are several ISO 64 reversal emulsions. Unlike Kodachrome, most are processed in E-6 or E6 compatible chemistry. E6 processing is readily available, often with fast turn around times. Slowest of the colour negative emulsions are the fine grain ISO 100 films. Bottom speed in black and white film is a slow ISO 25 (Agfapan 25), followed closely by Technical Pan film (ISO 32). Both monochrome and colour reversal films can be uprated to several times their normal speed. Compensation for what is in effect under-exposure is made during processing. In the case of E6 films, this takes place during the first developer stage, with black and white films, by the use of a speed increasing developer.

ADVANTAGES
Slow films give the best sharpness and detail, the finest grain, and are most suitable for making large prints. Slow colour slide film (above) also gives the most saturated colour and has the best latitude to exposure errors.

DISADVANTAGES
Because slow films require more exposure there is increased risk of camera shake and less potential for action shots in poor light. Slow black and white and colour films may also be rather high in contrast in bright sunlight.

FAST FILMS

Fast films (ISO 400 and upwards) are highly sensitive to light. They allow very fast shutter speeds for stopping action, normal shutter speeds for hand-held photographs in low light and flash exposures are often possible from up to 10 metres away.

There are lots of different fast films to choose from. At the bottom of the range, ISO 400 is available in colour print, colour slide and black and white emulsion. Faster, for tungsten shooting, is 3M's 640T (ISO 640). Top of the colour slide and print speed range for several film manufacturers are their ISO 1000 films. Faster still, from Fuji, are two ISO 1600 films (slide and print films). Staying in the slide line-up, Kodak have a variable speed Ektachrome film with an ISO 800-1600 speed rating which may also be uprated to ISO 3200. (Whatever the rating, the entire film must be exposed at the selected speed.) On the fast black and white film front, Kodak have Recording film (2475, ISO 1000) and Royal-X Pan which has a speed rating of ISO 1250.

ADVANTAGES
Pictures which cannot be taken with slow or medium speed films are often possible with fast film. Regardless of the light or weather, you are assured of the shortest possible exposure. The picture above was taken on a cloudy day but the ISO 400 colour negative film used permitted a shutter speed of 1/1000 to freeze movement. Fast colour negative films also cope well with different types of light – daylight, tungsten light or even fluorescent tube light – without producing a particularly pronounced colour cast.

DISADVANTAGES
All fast films produce grainy looking pictures and have a limited ability to show very fine detail. Colour negative ISO 400 films are surprisingly good, and apart from graininess the only problem may be harsh colours in sunlight and inability to cope with high contrast. Colour slides on ISO 400 film may suffer some loss in definition. Fast black and white films can give greyer results. Latitude for exposure error is good with black and white and colour negative types, but not so good with colour slide film.

Putting film through the camera

A wrongly loaded camera is worse than no camera at all. Although the film is loaded, you could be taking no pictures, or taking 36 shots on one single frame. Once the film is inside the camera it can be hard to tell if all is well. You can't open the back to look. So correct loading is vital.

Taking the mishaps in order, the first thing to watch is that the film is actually engaged on the sprocket holes as you close the camera back. Many photographers, even experienced ones, have made a mistake at this early stage, only to discover that there is no film to rewind when the counter reaches the last frame.

To avoid the mishap, always watch the rewind lever as you wind on the first frames. As the film feeds through to the next frame, the rewind lever should move too. If it doesn't the film is not engaged on the sprocket holes.

More camera accidents happen during loading or unloading than at any other time. So, the first thing is to find a safe place to change films: a table-top, car seat or other clean surface. (Some outfit cases are good for resting the camera on.)

More vulnerable still to mishaps at this stage are reloadable cassettes. These are loaded with short lengths of film from bulk reels. Their main attraction is the saving in film costs – buying in bulk reduces this considerably. However, unless care is taken, the likelihood of tramline marks on the film due to trapped dust or partial fogging due to the build-up of static during loading cannot be ruled out.

Make sure the exposed roll of film is fully wound back before you open the camera back, and avoid touching the shutter while loading.

Finally, if you do open the camera back and discover a forgotten film in the camera, close it again immediately. That way, if the lighting is not too bright, some of the frames may be salvaged.

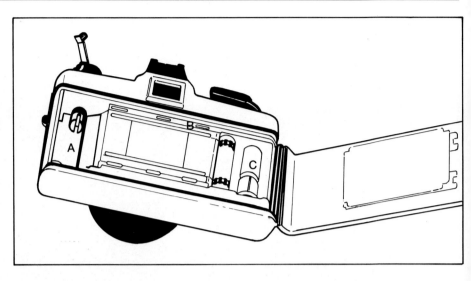

LOADING THE CAMERA
When loading the camera, always work in the shade – preferably indoors. This minimizes the chances of bright light leaking through the velvet light-trap on the cassette and fogging the film. Lift the rewind crank.
Hold the cassette with the opening pointing downwards. Now insert the tongue of the film firmly into the take-up spool (C).
When this is gripped by the teeth, gently pull the cassette across the shutter and drop it in the chamber (A).

ENGAGING THE FILM
Tighten the take-up spool gently until the film leader sprocket holes engage the sprocket drive teeth. Make sure that both sides are engaged and that the film is accurately located between the guide rails (B).
Close the back and wind the film on twice, releasing the shutter for blank frames. Winding on only once risks a fogged shot or two.
As soon as you have loaded the film set the ISO speed on the dial, and set the frame counter to 1.

REWINDING THE FILM
Never try to rewind a film without first depressing the rewind clutch release button (above), usually on the camera base.
Rewind slowly and smoothly and never try to overcome resistance (some cassettes may be stiff but there is a lot of difference between this and a jammed film). Turn the rewind knob clockwise. If you turn it the other way the film may be badly scratched and will be in the cassette emulsion-side out, risking more scratches later.

ALWAYS WIND BACK SLOWLY
Fast rewinding is to be avoided at all costs. Apart from a much greater risk of any dust particles getting drawn into the cassette and scratching the film, static electricity can be produced, attracting more dust and sometimes even making marks on the film. Another reason for slow rewinding is that when you reach the point that the leader parts company with the take-up spool, you should hear a click as it leaves the slot. Open the camera back now and the leader will still be sticking out of the cassette. This makes processing much easier. If in doubt, however, wind back fully, then there is no risk of too much film sticking out and spoiling your last frame.

HOME STORAGE OF FILM
Most films should be stored in a cool, dry place. If the weather is very hot you can keep film in a fridge – but let it warm up for two hours before you open the foil or plastic container. Otherwise there is a danger of condensation forming in the cassette.

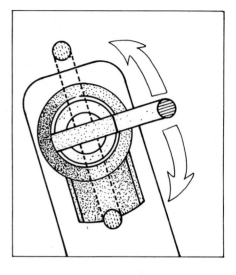

TAKE UP THE SLACK
If you have sudden doubts about whether your film is winding on correctly it is fairly easy to check. First, tighten the film in the cassette by winding back the rewind knob clockwise (see A above). Do not press the rewind release button on the bottom of the camera. You are not rewinding, just taking up any slack inside the cassette. As soon as you feel any resistance, stop winding. Noise from the cassette may indicate that you are over-tightening and rubbing the spooled film – risking scratch marks.

WIND ON AND WATCH
Having taken up the slack, take your next shot.
Now wind on as normal. As you wind on, watch the rewind knob to make sure that it is turning. If it turns anti-clockwise (see B above) then the film is being transported correctly.
After this, periodic glances at the rewind knob should show that it turns with winding on.
Most experienced photographers tend to keep an eye on the rewind knob all the time.

FRAME COUNTER PROBLEMS
Sometimes the film appears to reach its end before the frame counter shows 20, 24 or 36. There are four possible reasons for this: a) you have loaded a shorter film than you thought b) you have lost frames by winding on too much film when loading; c) the frame counter is faulty; d) the film is jammed.
Try turning the rewind knob in both directions (see C above). If you can move more than half a turn either way there is still film in the cassette. Rewind, unload and check the camera.

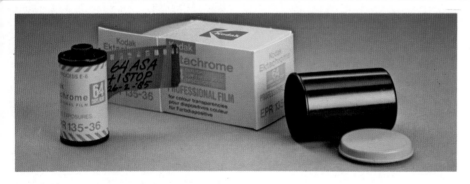

IDENTIFYING USED FILM
One of the worst disasters that can befall a photographer is to reload a roll of film that has already been exposed – thereby effectively ruining two sets of pictures at once.
There are two ways of avoiding this danger:
a) rewind the film fully, so that the leader is wound right back inside the cassette, making it impossible to reload the film;
b) tear off the leader after rewinding the film.
However, as leaving the leader out makes processing the film easier, it is preferable to mark the leader and/or the cassette clearly with felt-tip pen so that an exposed film is immediately identifiable.
Every box of film should have an expiry date coded or stamped somewhere on it.
With black and white film this may be four years ahead, but with colour, only one or two.
This is the date before which the film should be used to ensure that you get optimum results.

AFTER EXPOSURE
Always get your film processed as quickly as possible. Make sure that you mark all films clearly with your name and address.
Mark any special processing instructions on a label and wrap tightly round the cassette with a rubber band.

Starting an SLR outfit

Many picture opportunities are lost because of lighting problems, subject size or distance, and lack of camera support. A basic outfit of accessories helps to solve these commonly-met difficulties, and extends creative possibilities.

Lighting problems occur daily – or nightly. The most convenient solution is to use flash. This freezes movement, precludes camera shake and provides light totally independent of existing sources.

Camera shake can be eliminated by using a tripod.

Space and distance, closely related to subject size, can be tackled by using additional lenses.

Colour and tone can be improved and controlled by the use of filters.

Special effects, such as multiple images or soft focus, can be produced by lens attachments. You can start with a basic outfit and gradually add extra items as required.

THE BASIC OUTFIT
The flashgun can be carried or mounted on the camera. The tripod will hold a normal SLR firmly.
Which filters you include is up to you.

Close-up lenses and extension tubes increase close-focus capability. Telephoto lenses magnify distant subjects and wide angle lenses gather in wider views.

FILTERS
A filter is a piece of flat glass, or plastic, which screws into, or slips over, the front rim of a lens. A filter can be clear, slightly tinted or strongly coloured or even patterned.
The function of any filter is to control the way the tone or colour of a subject appears on the film.
With black and white, tone is important. With colour film, either negative or transparency, colour is crucial.
By fitting a filter to your lens you can effectively alter the contrast or colour balance of your subject to get the best results. The filters you use will depend on your personal preference and the kind of pictures you take.

FILTERS FOR BLACK AND WHITE
Without a filter (top) the film sees blue sky and white clouds as equal tones. Fit a yellow filter, and the tones become contrasted (above).

HAZE FILTERS
The effect of atmospheric haze in a landscape is to reduce the intensity of colour (top). Fitting a UV-Haze filter (above) helps cure the problem.

ACCESSORIES FOR LOW LIGHT
Suitable accessories allow you to overcome the problems associated with low light levels – camera shake, subject movement and long exposures.

USE A TRIPOD. . .
A tripod allows you to use a slow shutter speed without risking camera shake. You can then select an aperture and preserve the natural light.

. . .OR A FLASH GUN
Flash light can freeze movement and is suitable for use in daylight. But direct flash gives hard shadows and restricts choice of aperture.

THE LONG FOCUS LENS
When your subject is too far away to be a reasonable size in the frame, and you can't get any nearer, a long focus or telephoto lens is the answer.

This type of lens gives a magnified image compared with a normal lens. A 200mm telephoto, for instance, would give an image four times as large as the standard 50mm when used the same distance away.

Long focus lenses are ideal for sports events where it is difficult to get close to the players; for candid shots when you don't want to go too close with your camera for fear of intruding and spoiling the spontaneity; and for shots of animals which may be frightened away by the approach of a photographer.

THE WIDE ANGLE LENS
A wide angle lens has a greater angle of view (ie it takes more in, top and bottom and each side) than the standard 50mm lens.

What a 50mm lens can get into the frame area from, say, 6 metres away, a 24mm wide angle will be able to get in from about 3 metres away.

This makes the wide angle lens useful for working in confined spaces, especially interiors.

Wide angle lenses also have a far greater depth of field than a standard lens. This makes them particularly suitable for shots like the one above which benefit from being in sharp focus throughout as great an area of the frame as possible.

CLOSE-UP ACCESSORIES
Normal lenses focus to around 50cm. Many subjects, such as flowers, are still too far away for you to fill the frame with them, even at this distance. Close-up accessories bring closer the near limit for focusing, and enable the subject to be recorded life-size.

There are two main accessories: close-up lenses, which act like magnifying glasses fixed in front of the camera lens; and extension tubes, which fit between the lens and the camera, and so extend the outward focusing movement of the lens.

Both are easily and quickly fitted and are portable. In good light they are ideal for taking pictures of flowers (above) and insects.

Telephoto lenses and converters

Almost all SLR cameras have lenses that can be separated from the body of the camera. This means that you can change from one lens to another without having to change cameras or film.

The standard lens on most 35mm SLRs is the 50mm. It is sometimes called the human vision lens, because the area of a subject that it records on film is roughly the same as the amount of a scene taken in by the human eye.

This is fine if you simply want to record what you see. But there may be times when you wish you could record part of the picture in greater detail without having to approach nearer to the subject. This is when a change to a lens of longer focus is particularly useful.

A long focus, or telephoto, lens gives a bigger image on film than the 50mm. With the subject at a set distance from the camera a 100mm lens, for example, will give an image twice the size of that given by a 50mm.

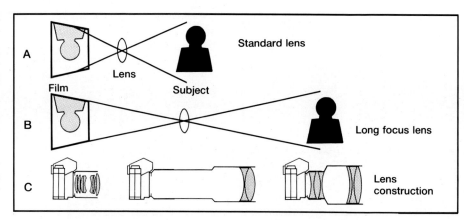

THE LONG FOCUS LENS
A basic long focus lens simply extends the distance between the glass elements of the lens and the film plane. It is this increased distance which gives the magnified image.

Diagrams A and B in the illustration above show that by increasing this distance (known as the focal length) a long focus lens will produce an image of a distant subject the same size as that produced by a shorter focus lens much closer to the subject enabling you to alter the scale without changing your position. This means that with a long focus lens you can get greater detail without having to get any closer.

TELEPHOTO DESIGN
As with the long focus lens, the telephoto gives a larger image on film than the 50mm from the same distance. There is obviously a limit to the physical length of a lens. So, to reduce the bulk of long focus lenses, the telephoto construction is used. Extra optical elements take the place of the extra length.

This is shown simply in diagram C above. On the left is a standard lens, in the centre a long focus lens, and on the right a telephoto of the same focal length. Some telephoto lenses are less than half the length they would be if they were of simple long focus construction.

THE 100mm PORTRAIT LENS
The 100mm telephoto gives an image twice the size of a standard 50mm. It is often called a portrait lens because it is ideal for this kind of picture. Most lenses of this focal length are compact. Some are as fast (that is, have a wide maximum aperture) as 50mm lenses – with a maximum aperture of f2 or even f1·4. Optical quality is usually excellent.
It is also a fine selective lens for general shots, like the train above.

THE POPULAR 135mm
135mm may seem an odd focal length to be popular, compared with the 50mm, but it gives 2·7 × magnification while still being easy to use. Fairly distant subjects are pulled in (see above), yet you can still take a head and shoulders portrait in a normal room.
The maximum aperture is usually between f3·5 and f2·5, and it is about twice the length of a 50mm. The 135mm is one of the cheapest telephotos.

THE 200mm ACTION LENS
The 200mm gives 4 × magnification compared with the standard 50mm. This is equivalent to blowing up 1/16th of the normal picture area to fill the frame (see above). It is reasonably priced, easy to handle and will usually have a maximum aperture of about f3·5. It is an ideal outdoor sports lens. Most 200mm lenses do not focus much closer than 3 metres and are, therefore, usually unsuitable for use indoors.

TELEPHOTO CONVERTERS

One of the cheapest ways of adding a telephoto to your outfit is to buy a tele-converter.

A converter is far cheaper than a separate telephoto lens but performs much the same job. It fits between the SLR body and another lens. Normally the first lens you use with a tele-converter will be a 50mm. If you decide to buy other lenses later, it will work with these as well. The tele-converter effectively extends the focal length of a lens. A 2 × converter doubles the focal length (50mm becomes 100mm). A 3 × converter trebles it (50mm becomes 150mm).

CONVERTERS AND EXPOSURE

When using a tele-converter, exposure must be increased. This is because although the amount of light from the subject remains the same whatever lens is used, with a converter fitted it has to cover a greater area of film. A 2 × converter magnifies the image to twice the size, but 4 times the area, so it must receive 4 times as much light (an exposure increase of 2 stops). The picture above was taken with a 50mm lens. For the right-hand picture a 2 × converter was added. Exposure was increased by 2 stops. The diagram on the right shows the positioning of the converter.

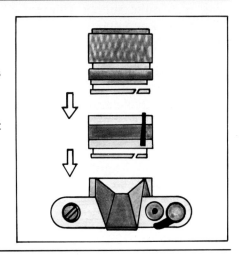

DISADVANTAGES OF TELEPHOTO

Telephoto lenses need more careful focusing than standard lenses, are harder to hold steadily, and camera shake (above) shows up strongly. In fact, any faults which might occur with a 50mm are magnified along with the size of the subject. Maximum aperture is not a problem with today's fast films, but don't hesitate to use a wide enough f stop to avoid having to use slow shutter speeds.

ADVANTAGES

Telephotos are selective and help to eliminate unwanted surroundings and you can take pictures without being noticed. Their shallow depth of field can throw unwanted backgrounds out of focus, but take care to avoid shots like the one above. The more distant viewpoint used with a telephoto is more flattering to faces than close-up views. Noses especially, appear in better proportion.

FLATTER YOUR FRIENDS

This portrait was taken with a 100mm telephoto. Distracting background detail has been cut out because of the limited field of view and the slightly flattened perspective is flattering.

How to use long lenses

Lightweight, relatively inexpensive medium telephoto lenses and zooms are probably the first choice for long lenses. At focal lengths up to 200mm, they perform and handle quite like the 50mm standard lens. Over 200mm, telephoto lenses produce dramatic pictures – but they also require more care with technique. Experiment with teleconverters or binoculars.

Converters for use with any lens will turn medium telephotos into long ones quite simply. Convert a 200mm lens into 400mm with a × 2 converter or 600mm with a × 3 converter.

Binoculars allow you to take telephoto pictures with only a standard lens and a suitable adaptor. Use one barrel only, with the eyepiece about 1cm (½in) in front of the front element of the camera lens. The resulting focal length will be the length of the lens multiplied by the binoculars' power.

TELESCOPES
Unlike binoculars, telescopes have detachable eyepieces. This means that they can be fitted directly to an SLR. The greatest magnification comes from astronomical telescopes.

MIRROR LENSES
The picture above also shows a barrel-like lens: this is a long telephoto. It is called a mirror lens and is far more compact than a normal telephoto with focal lengths from 250-1000mm.

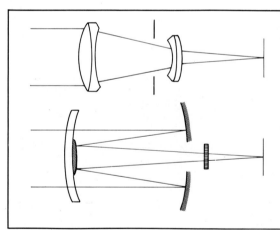

The telephoto lens has a special construction which allows it to be made much shorter than its actual focal length. This requires extra lens elements at the rear of the lens.

The mirror lenses uses mirrors to fold the light on its path through the lens barrel, as shown here. This requires a fat lens, but it can be made much shorter than a telephoto.

MIRROR LENSES VERSUS. . .
The choice between a mirror lens or a telephoto lens of the same focal length has various pros and cons. Mirror lenses are far lighter and easier to handle but they are about twice the price of orthodox telephotos. And cheap mirror lenses are less sharp than cheap normal telephotos. They are more vulnerable to rough handling and can be costly to repair. Most have a fixed f stop and require filters (fitted on the rear) to cut down light.

NORMAL TELEPHOTOS
Bulk and camera shake are the chief problems of long focal length lenses. If you need to use one regularly, this can be important. They are less delicate and the weight can make them easier to hold steady. They have variable apertures – a 400mm f6·3 lens stops down to f22 or even f32 – and they are faster to focus. Price is another factor you will need to consider. You may be able to buy two telephotos of quality for the price of one mirror lens.

DOUGHNUT EFFECTS
The design of the mirror lens makes doughnut shaped rings appear in out-of-focus highlights (as above). This only shows up in sparkling highlights, and can be used as a creative effect.

SUPPORTING A LONG LENS
A 500mm lens covers an angle of just under 5°. A photographer with a shaky hand may easily hold a lens so unsteadily that it moves more than 5° when the shutter is released, and the picture will show severe camera shake. Hold long lenses very firmly and securely, using the highest possible shutter speed to cut down the shake. A pistol grip or shoulder stock (shown above) makes aiming more reliable. If the subject is still, use a tripod or lean on a wall or car for steadiness. Choose a fast film to maximize the telephoto's shallow depth of field.

FOLLOWING ACTION
Panning the camera round with a moving target allows you to use slower shutter speeds, giving a blurred background as above. Follow through your pan after releasing the shutter.

SHARPNESS AND DEPTH
At wider apertures, only a little of the subject depth will be in sharp focus. Remember that one-third of the depth of field is in front of the point of focus and two-thirds is behind it.

LONG TELE DATA

Recommended shutter speeds

300mm	1/250	minimum
400mm	1/500	minimum
500mm	1/500	minimum
600mm	1/500	minimum
800mm	1/1000	minimum
1000mm	1/1000	minimum
1250mm	1/1000	minimum
1600mm	1/2000	minimum
2000mm	1/2000	minimum

Angles of view (35 mm)

300mm	8°
400mm	6°
500mm	5°
1000mm	2·5°
2000mm	1·25°

SHOOTING FOR THE MOON
The full moon is a very appealing subject to owners of very long telephoto lenses. The whole moon can be shot with short exposures at medium apertures. A telescope with a focal length of about 2000mm will give a good image size. To fill the frame with either the sun or the moon, you will need 3000mm. With ISO 100 film, you should give an exposure of 1/125 at f8.
Do not use long exposures since the moon is imperceptibly moving and will, therefore, show blur.

PHOTOGRAPHING SUNSETS
The effects of a telephoto lens are at their most dramatic when you are taking sunset pictures.
To get the sun's disc as large as in the picture above, you will need a 500mm lens.

33

Wide angle lenses and converters

Just as lenses of a longer focal length select part of a view and enlarge it to fill the 35mm frame, lenses with a shorter focal length reduce the scale of image detail and take in a wider view. They are called wide angle lenses.

To take an example, a 24mm wide angle gives an image half the size of that of a 50mm. But the area of the subject will be four times as great.

It is this increased angle of view (hence wide angle) which is the greatest advantage of a wide angle lens. If you are working in a confined space, say a room, it enables you to take in much more of a subject than you could with a 50mm.

Another characteristic of a wide angle lens is that it has greater depth of field. Even at wide apertures the subject can be sharp throughout the picture area. This means that you can focus on an object quite close to the camera and still be sure that the view beyond will be in focus.

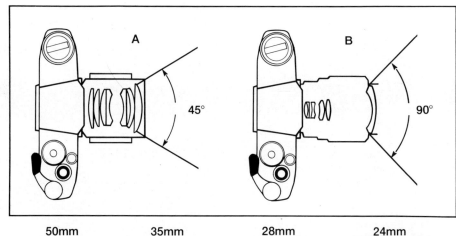

50mm

35mm

28mm

24mm

ANGLE OF VIEW
Diagram above shows the angle of view of a 50mm lens (A) and a 24mm (B). 24mm is ½ the focal length of the 50mm and has 2 × the angle of view.

POPULAR FOCAL LENGTHS
The most popular wide angles are shown above. Next to a 50mm, a 35mm is often smaller, a 28mm about the same size, and a 24mm usually larger.

THE 35mm SHORT STANDARD
Although the 35mm lens is a wide angle, it is no harder to use than a 50mm lens, and can often replace it. The 35mm is an ideal all-rounder. The extra 40% included in the picture means you can photograph small groups indoors, take full-length portraits without standing too far back, and include buildings from reasonable distances. Most flashguns are capable of covering the view of a 35mm lens.

THE 28mm: AN IDEAL COMPROMISE
The 28mm lens is a good first choice of wide angle to add to your SLR and 50mm lens. Pictures have a definite wide appearance. The 28mm allows full-length shots in small rooms, sweeping landscapes with lots of sky, and interesting close-up effects. Many flashguns, however, need a special attachment to spread their light over the wide area taken in by the 28mm lens.

THE 24mm: AN ULTRA-WIDE
For dramatic wide angle effects often seen in professional photographs, the 24mm is ideal. It is a favourite lens for the architectural, landscape, news and creative scenic photographer. It is not suitable for everyday pictures as it needs a great deal of care in use. This kind of wide angle may seem to stretch objects near the corners of the picture into elongated shapes. Special guns or attachments may be needed for flash.

WIDE ANGLE CONVERTERS

A wide angle converter screws in the front filter thread of the 50mm just like a lens hood or filter. They normally have adaptor rings so that if you change your SLR, the converter can fit the new standard lens. A typical converter (shown above) will turn a 50mm into a wide angle equivalent of a 35mm. Fitted to a 28mm the result is a 20mm ultra-wide view. The f stops marked on the lens still apply, but you will have to focus through the viewfinder. Fitting a converter lets you focus much closer.

TYPES OF CONVERTER

There are two types of converter. One gives a sharp image with straight lines like a normal wide angle, but corners may be slightly blurred. The other, called a semi-fisheye converter, turns straight lines into curves. Both types can be fitted to other lenses as well as the 50mm. The picture above shows a scene taken with a 50mm lens. The shot above right was taken from the same spot but a 2 × straight line converter was added. The diagram, right, shows the positioning.

DISADVANTAGES

Using a wide angle calls for care. The two shots above are typical of bad wide angle pictures. To get a reasonable-sized image on the film you need to be closer with a wide angle. Compose your shots deliberately. The shot above right shows what happens if you move closer but don't think. Children have to be photographed from their own level. Aim down and you get this ugly effect.

ADVANTAGES

The big advantage of any wide angle is that you can include subjects without missing parts off, even in tight situations. The subject may be lost in the frame, but it is always possible to crop or enlarge it later.

Wide angles also need less critical focusing (you see this when you look through the viewfinder), and more of the depth of the picture is sharp at any given aperture.

WORKING WITH WIDES

The good qualities of a wide angle lens come out in this picture. The lines of the subject, the sky, the viewpoint and strong perspective all work well together.

Zoom lenses: the one-lens outfit

One big drawback of interchangeable lenses is that they have to be changed. To get a different field of view you have to remove one lens and fit another. If the subject moves or the light changes while you do this, the picture is lost.

Another problem is the jump between one focal length and the next. You may own a 50mm standard lens and a 135mm telephoto. But a particular shot could need an 85mm lens for the best composition if you cannot change position.

To overcome these problems, the zoom, or variable focal length lens, can take the place of three separate lenses (in many cases) and fill the gaps between.

In addition to focus and f stop controls there is a third setting – focal length. This can be changed to provide exactly the required focal length between the marked minimum and maximum.

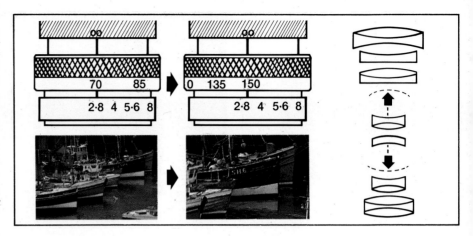

ZOOM RANGES
The longest and shortest focal lengths are always marked on a zoom and these are used to describe the lens. Often they are unusual: you can buy a 35-70mm zoom, for example, but not separate lenses for the lengths in between.
The ratio of a zoom is the difference in the magnification from the shortest to longest setting. A 70-210mm is a 3 to 1 zoom: at 210mm the image is three times as large as at 70mm.

ZOOM OPERATION
The diagrams above show the controls of a twin-ring zoom, set on 70mm (left) and 150mm (centre). Note the change in magnification of the image. This type of zoom has a separate zooming ring. Another type is the one-touch zoom, which combines the zoom control and focusing ring. The right-hand diagram shows how the middle elements of the lens move as the zoom control is operated.

WIDE ANGLE ZOOMS
Wide-angle zoom lenses are popular, although they are quite expensive, and can be very large and heavy. Nearly all wide angle zooms go up to around 50mm maximum focal length, so they can be used in place of the standard lens. There are several 28-50mm zooms which are the same size as a normal 50mm lens, but limited to f3·5 or f4·5 maximum aperture. Sometimes the maximum f stop changes from one end of the range to the other – this is marked f3·5-4·5 28-50mm, meaning that although f3·5 is available at 28mm, at 50mm you are limited to f4·5. Wide angle zooms are ideal if you do a lot of landscape or architectural (both inside and out) photography. The shot above left was taken with a 28-50mm wide angle zoom lens.

MID-RANGE ZOOMS
Some cameras are sold with a zoom lens as an alternative to the standard 50mm lens. Standard or mid-range zooms are ideal if you want only one lens. A typical range would be 35-70mm – from wide angle to portrait. The disadvantages, compared with a normal 50mm lens, are loss of quality, higher cost, extra size and weight, and limited aperture (some are f2·8 but most are f3·5). Many have close-up controls. If you decide to change to a mid-range zoom in place of your standard lens, check carefully that the normal focusing range is good enough. Sometimes the focusing stops at 1·5 or even 2 metres unless you use the close-up control. The shots above (centre and right) were taken at either limit of a 45-90mm zoom. Mid-range zooms are ideal for family photographs.

TELE-ZOOMS

Telephoto zooms (used for the shot above) get rid of the need to carry more than one bulky long lens. A 70-210 zoom is usually about the same size as a 300mm telephoto. An 80-200mm zoom, with a slightly smaller range, will be the same size as a 200mm. Most tele-zooms cover up to 200mm and have a ratio of 2·5:1 to 3·5:1. Typical ranges also include 50-200mm, 85-300mm and 100-300mm lenses.

PORTRAIT ZOOMS

If you do not want such a large range of focal lengths or such a powerful tele magnification, a portrait zoom is much smaller. These usually have a range of either 70 or 75mm to 150mm. A few run from 50mm to 135mm and even to 200mm. Set on the maximum limit, shots like the one above are perfectly possible. If more power is needed, most makes let you fit a teleconverter to further extend telephoto limits.

CLOSE FOCUSING

Many zoom lenses have a close focusing or macro facility, which lets you take close-up shots (see picture above) without extension tubes or extra lenses. In some zooms the focus control is extended so you get continuous focusing down to under 1m. On other lenses, a button or twisting ring control alters the zoom action to a focusing action, so instead of zooming, the lens focuses very close.

CREATIVE ZOOM EFFECTS

Zooms open a world of creative chances. With a zoom you can adjust the composition precisely – no compromise is needed. By changing viewpoint and focal length you can get exactly the shot you want. Dramatic creative effects are also possible. One of the most popular of these is to zoom during a long exposure. You turn the zoom from short focal length to long rather than vice-versa. This gives a streaked image which seems to rush out of the picture towards the edges.

EXPOSURE

In the shot above, the normal scene (left) was converted to the zoom effect using a mid-range zoom. By stopping down to f22 and using slow film, an exposure of ¼ second was possible in daylight. The zoom control was moved from 40mm to 80mm.

WHEN TO START ZOOMING

If you try this effect, support the camera firmly. Use a tripod. The best results are obtained if you start the zoom just after the shutter opens, so that part of the subject stays sharp. Experiment with moving subjects too. Results look best in colour.

37

Equipment for close-up pictures

One of the great advantages of the camera is that it can take an area of detail and isolate it from an overall scene. A photograph of this detail can then be studied at leisure, without the distraction of the original surroundings.

However, if you want a small subject to fill the frame you run into problems with your standard 50mm lens. The focusing range of most 50mm lenses extends from infinity to about half a metre, so that only those parts of a subject more than half a metre away can be recorded in focus.

The solution is to use special close-up equipment, and this is particularly suited to SLR cameras. You can see through the lens and through any close-up attachments, so focusing and careful framing is easy. Any SLR can be used with close-up attachments and most of the equipment is simple and reasonably cheap.

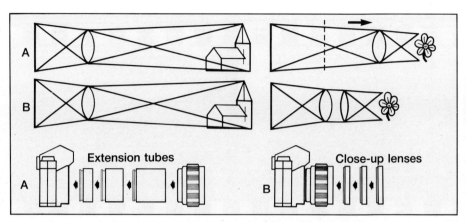

MOVING THE LENS
As you move the focusing ring of any SLR to closer distances, the front of the lens moves outwards. The further the lens moves away from the film the closer you can focus. Every lens has its focusing limit, but you can extend this on an SLR by using extension tubes. These are rings which when placed between the lens and the camera body extend the distance between the lens and the film. They are usually sold in sets of three and can be used singly or in combination for much closer focusing.

ADDING MORE LENSES
The diagrams above show the two main ways of getting a close-up. You can either (A) take your lens closer to the subject; or (B) you can magnify the image. With your standard 50mm lens you can magnify the image by attaching close-up lenses. These screw into the front of the lens and work like a magnifying glass. They are marked in diopter strengths. One diopter focuses at 100cm away, two diopters at half that distance (50cm), three diopters at one third (33·3cm) and so on.

USING EXTENSION TUBES
Extension tubes are harder to use than close-up lenses but allow closer, sharper pictures. Because the lens is moved closer to the subject, less light reaches the film. The finder image is also dimmer so compensation is needed if you use a manual camera or flash. Extension tubes are bulky and can be expensive. You must remove and refit the camera lens to use them (see above). The focusing distance depends on the focal length of the lens used. A 12mm extension tube has very little effect on a telephoto lens, a moderate effect on a 50mm lens, and the strongest effect of all on a wide angle lens.

CAMERA COUPLINGS
Unlike the close-up lens, extension tubes break the link between the lens and the camera. Auto extension tubes have couplings to overcome this. Make sure that the auto tubes you buy match your SLR.

FOCUSING WITH TUBES
In close-ups with tubes, moving the focusing ring of the lens has little effect on focusing because the depth of field is very limited. Focus by moving the camera backwards and forwards. The picture above was taken with tubes.

USING CLOSE-UP LENSES

Close-up lenses (CUs) are easy to use. They screw in like filters and have no effect on exposure. The focus distance is determined by the power of the close-up lens, not by the lens you fit it on. A 3 diopter (+3) close-up lens will set the focusing distance at 33·3cm, whether you use it on a 200mm lens or a 50mm. The focusing image in the SLR finder is bright when close-up lenses are used. They are pocketable, and can be bought singly. You do not need to remove the camera lens to fit one. In theory they take the edge off picture sharpness, but this can be ignored for most photographs (see above).

POWERS OF LENSES

Popular CU lens strengths are +1, +2 and +3 diopters. The first has little effect. A +2 gives distances of 50cm and closer. It is ideal for extending the range of many lenses which have a close focus limit of 50cm, giving an unbroken range. A +3 gives distances 33·3cm and closer, but if your lens does not focus this close already, a +3 will leave a gap. The full set of three CUs lets you focus on any distance down to about 12cm with most cameras. The shot above is a typical +2 diopter close-up.

USING TWO TOGETHER

CU lenses can be used together for closer distances. The picture above was taken with a 50mm lens. The distance scale on the lens was set to its closest focus of 50cm. Two close-up lenses, +3 and +1 (total +4), were then added, giving a focusing distance of 25cm from the front of the lens. On a 35mm negative this would give an image of about ⅕ life-size.

CLOSE-UP LENS PROBLEMS

1) Normal close-up lenses are so limited in magnifying power that several may be needed together for very small subjects. Use too many and you get vignetting, as above.
2) Picture quality suffers at the edges with close-up lenses. Using two or three together can increase flare if shooting into the light.
3) If you have lenses with different filter threads you may need two sets of close-up lenses.

EXTENSION TUBE PROBLEMS

1) Extension tubes made for use with the standard 50mm lens may not be very convenient with others. For example, you may want to focus closer with a wide angle but find you get the blurred result above.
2) Some wide aperture 50mm lenses (f1·4 or f1·2) give pictures badly blurred at the edges when used with tubes.
3) Tubes are not very flexible. With some lenses, none of the three tubes in a set will give the distance you want.

ZOOM CLOSE-UPS

For about the same price as a set of cheaper extension tubes you can buy a special zoom close-up lens. Using two glass elements, a variable close-up lens like that above has a range of +1 to +10 diopters (100cm to 10cm focus), with no gaps. It seems a good answer to problems, but the picture quality is usually poor. The edges are blurred, and at +10 power, cut-off occurs. With variable close-up lenses a small aperture like f16 is vital.

Ultra close-up photography

Normal close-up lenses and extension tubes are easy to use to take good pictures of fairly small, close-up subjects. But when you want to get really detailed shots of very small subjects you may need more. Macro equipment is harder to use than ordinary close-up equipment, but it is more versatile.

Macro photographs need very good light and you will require small apertures to keep the subject sharply in focus so you will also need a steady tripod.

Magnification of the subject in a photograph should be related to the negative or slide size, not the size of the print or the projected image. Life-size images are described as 1:1, half life-size 1:2, twice life-size 2:1 and so on. These are called reproduction ratios and can be important in the exposure calculations you need to make.

REVERSING THE LENS
The cheapest way to take sharp macro photographs is to fix your lens on to the camera back to front. This only works with standard or wide angle lenses. A special adaptor ring, known as a reversing ring (shown above), screws or bayonets into the lens throat. The lens is screwed on to this using the front filter thread. The lens is now further from the film and focuses extremely close-up. The reversed optical arrangement helps to keep the picture sharp from corner to corner.

MACRO LENSES
Lenses which focus very close without the help of extension tubes or bellows are called macro lenses. They can also be used for distant shots and focus to infinity. They are corrected for close-ups so results are much sharper at the edges of the field than with ordinary lenses or close-up accessories. Most macro lenses for 35mm cameras have focal lengths in the 50-100mm range. Maximum aperture is fairly wide. Focusing is normally to half life-size or life-size.

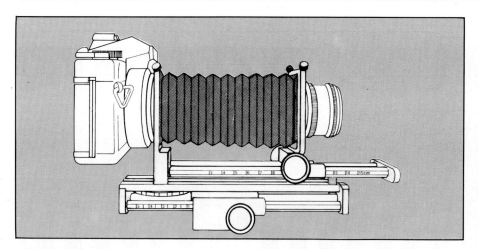
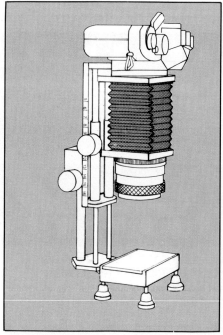

MACRO BELLOWS
For bigger-than-life-size magnification you can buy bellows that fit between the camera and the lens. They act like extension tubes but better. You can extend them to any point within their range, rather than having to progress in fixed steps.

Simple bellows are cheap but do not have couplings to stop down the lens automatically. The best bellows retain full metering functions with many extra features. Use them with a reversed standard lens, a macro lens or – for high magnification – a reversed macro.

FOCUSING RAILS
At very close distances it is easier to focus by moving the camera backwards or forwards than with the focusing ring. (If you are using a reversed lens, you will not be able to use the focusing ring at all.)

Focusing the lens alters the magnification, which can be extremely critical with macro pictures. Focusing rails as shown in the diagram above fit between the camera and the tripod: turning the knob moves the whole assembly (camera and bellows) for fine positioning.

FOCUSING STANDS
Macro stands (shown above) hold the camera vertically like a microscope for easy table-top use. The subject is held on a flat specimen stage. This is ideal for photographing small objects like stamps or coins.

REPRODUCTION RATIOS

Most macro lenses and some bellows are engraved with reproduction ratios. With bellows, these take account of what lens you are using. For example, one scale is marked for use with a 50mm lens and one for a 100mm lens. The picture above was taken with a 50mm lens and bellows extended to 25mm. This gave a reproduction ratio of 1:2 (half life-size). With ISO 400 film, the exposure required was 1/500 at f8, a good speed and aperture for a hand held exposure with a close subject.

EXPOSURE

This life-size (1:1 ratio) picture was taken with the same 50mm lens and 50mm of extension. This extra extension makes the image dimmer because the lens is further from the film. The lens was left on f8 for this shot, but because one extra stop of light was lost in the extra bellows extension the exposure time had to be increased to 1/250. Through-the-lens metering will cope with this automatically, as will an automatic exposure camera. Set the smallest aperture you can for good depth of field.

DEPTH OF FIELD SHUTTER SPEEDS

The more you magnify the image, the less depth of field is available. In this twice life-size picture (2:1 ratio) only a couple of millimeters from front to back is sharp. With the 100mm of bellows extension needed, exposure was 1/60 at f8. To get more depth of field, you would need to set a smaller aperture and a correspondingly slower shutter speed but then, even with a tripod, the slightest camera shake or subject movement will be recorded so flash is normally needed to freeze the subject.

EXPOSURE INCREASES AT MACRO MAGNIFICATIONS

As the lens is moved further from the film by extension, the image becomes dimmer. This table gives approximate exposure compensations with a 50mm lens.

Extension	Repro ratio	Increase in exposure
20mm	1:2	1 stop
50mm	1:1	2 stops
100mm	3:2	3 stops
150mm	2:1	4 stops
200mm	3:1	5 stops

To calculate the true aperture at any extension – when you are using a hand held light meter, or when you are working with flash – use this formula. Add the focal length of the lens to the extension of the bellows (from the front of the camera to the back of the lens). Divide this by the lens focal length. Then multiply the aperture that is set on the lens by the result, ie:

$$\text{True f stop} = \frac{\text{focal length} + \text{extension}}{\text{focal length}} \times \text{f stop}$$

MANUAL FLASH

With automatic flash guns, the sensor is unreliable at distances as close as the one needed for the shot of these crystals.
Use manual flash, working out the exposure by trial and error. Start at the closest distance on the scale and work down, bracketing your exposures.

POSITIONING FLASH

Since you lose light with extension attachments, you can gain light by positioning the flashgun nearer the subject.
If you fix the gun to the lens itself, the flashgun is automatically brought closer to the subject as the extension becomes progressively longer.

Completing your SLR outfit

With your SLR camera, lenses, filters and close-up accessories you have an outfit – a system. All the items combine to make a working kit to tackle many different subjects and conditions.

At this stage, the system is compact enough to carry around with you in its entirety, but you will need something to carry it all in. If not, you might be tempted to leave one or two items behind – a close-up lens is rarely needed when shooting motor racing, for example; a telephoto is probably of no use on a trip round the interior of a stately building. But there is nothing more frustrating than knowing you have the right equipment for a once-in-a-lifetime picture, but you have left it at home.

There are many types of camera case sold, from expensive aluminium to soft vinyl. Show your outfit to a dealer and he will usually have one to fit it. One idea is to cut a foam rubber case insert to take your own items of equipment.

CARRYING AND PROTECTING
The case above protects valuable equipment, as well as making it easy to carry. Proper camera outfit cases have soft linings and foam padding. Check that equipment fits snugly, is fairly evenly distributed and does not jostle.

WHAT SIZE OF CASE?
Don't buy the smallest case to fit your kit. Allow room in the case for the extra lens you may soon need. Bags with moveable dividers are versatile; ones with foam liners cut into shapes need new liners if the kit is changed later.

WHAT CAUSES FLARE?
Bright light from outside the picture area enters the camera lens and, instead of being focused on the film, it hits parts of the lens interior.
This can have two effects. If the source is large, like a bright sky, the reflected stray light puts a soft foggy veil over the whole picture (see above). If it is small, like a bright sun, spots of light (often hexagon-shaped because of the aperture) are scattered around.

LENS HOODS PREVENT FLARE
Compare the shot above with that on the left. For this shot a lens hood was fitted before taking the picture. The hood shields the lens from bright light coming from outside the picture area, but stops short of actually appearing in the frame itself. The best lens hoods are rectangular, to match the picture shape, but most are circular and therefore cheaper. Make sure the hood suits the lens.

TRIPOD AND CABLE RELEASE
Common sense accessories for available light photography of indoor subjects such as this church interior.

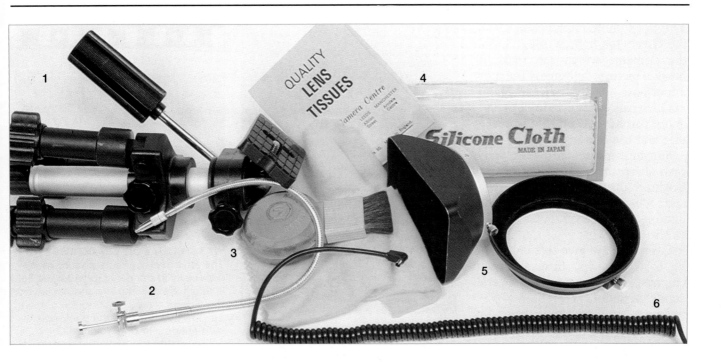

SHAKE-FREE ACCESSORIES
Your tripod (1) probably straps outside your case, but inside, carry a cable release (2). This connects to the camera and replaces the shutter button for tripod exposures. It is flexible and prevents camera shake when firing.

CLEANING THE KIT
Lenses collect dust, so carry a blower brush (3) to blow it off. Cleaning cloths (4) polish lenses but must be kept in dust-free bags. It is better to leave a filter on each lens and to clean that. Clean the camera body as well.

HOODS AND FLASH CABLE
Lens hoods (5) protect lenses and cut out stray light which causes flare. Each lens should have one. A long flash extension cable (6) lets you create dramatic lighting effects or cure red-eye problems easily.

FORMAL PORTRAITS
Tripods are used for portraiture to enable the photographer to attend to the sitter rather than the camera.

CREATIVE OFF-CAMERA FLASH
With a long extension cable for your flash, lots of interesting lighting effects are possible. You need to experiment for the best results. A long, uncoiled cable is cheapest and most versatile. You can also buy flash mounting shoes for fixing the flash to a tripod.
Always work out your exposures on flash-to-subject distance, not camera-to-subject, or use auto flash.

TRY THESE TECHNIQUES
Direct sidelight (above left): hold the flash a few feet to one side of a person's face, slightly in front.
Silhouette: stand the subject in front of a white background. Use flash on the background only and you get a pure black silhouette.
Inverted lighting: ask your subject to hold the flash at waist level and aim it up for dramatic portraits like that above.

How light affects your photographs

The word photography comes from the Greek for light writing. Of all the elements which can make or break a picture, lighting is the most important. In a studio a photographer can control light, but outdoors you have to be able to recognize and use existing light.

Sunshine gives a hard light which casts sharp shadows, makes colours brighter, throws texture into relief and, when used carefully as side-lighting, gives a pronounced 3-D effect.

Overcast days give soft light with no hard shadows, little ability to emphasize texture, and an overall gentle gradation.

Direct sun can come from the front, side or back of the subject, and in each case it will produce a totally different effect.

White clouds which do not obscure the sun make the light less hard, reducing the overall contrast.

KEEPING THE SUN BEHIND YOU
The picture above shows the kind of lighting often used by beginners. The shadows fall behind the subject, the light is evenly bright and detail good, but there is no modelling or texture.

WATCH OUT FOR SHADOWS
The time of day affects picture results, especially in the evening when the light is much lower in the sky and comes from the side or directly behind the camera. The low sun has cast the photographer's own shadow into the picture above. In some light this is almost inevitable unless you can aim the camera upwards or let the shadow fall in an already shaded area. Other nearby objects may also cast unwanted shadows in this kind of light.

PORTRAITS AND LIGHT
Lighting is important in portraiture as we like to see the shape, colour and texture of a person's face. But a harsh, accurate picture is rarely flattering – it shows up blemishes and lines. So unless you are taking a character study of a weatherbeaten face, deliberate sidelighting is ruled out.
You might expect over-the-shoulder light to work well for portraits, but look at the picture above. The subject's eyes are screwed up due to the glare. Although people usually also smile when they do this, the effect is tense.

REPOSITION THE SUBJECT
On a dull day there are no problems. But in sunshine you get a much better result (above) by moving your subject so that the sun is on her back. To lighten the now shaded face, use a light surface to bounce the light back.

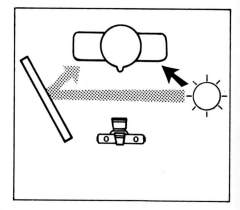

USING FILL-IN
Reflecting light onto the shaded parts of a subject is called fill-in. It works in much the same way as using a mirror to flash signals. You use a reflective surface to bounce the light in the direction you want it (see diagram above). Any reflective surface will have the same effect. A purpose-made silver reflector sheet is ideal, but you can use a newspaper, an open book or a convenient whitewashed wall. If you are shooting colour film don't use a coloured reflector, as the colour will be thrown on to the subject.

44

FRONT LIGHT IS TOO FLAT
One challenge of photography is to make three-dimensional subjects translate to two-dimensional paper. The main clues should be the texture and form of the subject. But direct, over-the-shoulder lighting, falling on the front of the subject is flat.
The picture above was taken with the light behind the camera. There is very little shadow on the bricks; they show hardly any texture and the whole image looks rather flat.

SIDELIGHT FOR TEXTURE
When the sun strikes the surface of a subject at an oblique angle, the effect of cross-lighting (see above) gives an impression of solidness and texture. To make the most of this effect you should expose for the highlights. That is, take a spot reading from one of the brightest parts of the subject. Cross, or side, lighting does not only occur in low sunlight. It is often obtained when the sun is high; the effect is then from top to bottom.

OVERCAST LIGHTING
Overcast light often has a greater modelling ability than flat sunlight. Even a totally overcast day has a strong overhead bias; completely flat results are only produced if the ground acts as a big reflector. Sand and snow can do this. The photograph above was taken under dull conditions, but there is still plenty of three-dimensional quality in the subject matter, and the absence of deep shadow makes it possible to see detail throughout the scene.

SHOOTING IN SILHOUETTE
By taking a photograph with the light coming from directly behind the subject you can obtain a silhouette. You take the exposure reading straight from the overall scene without making any correction for the strong light behind the subject. This will give a correctly exposed background but a subject in deep shadow.
Silhouettes can be a flattering way to take a portrait because they hide facial details, and more importantly, blemishes like lines and wrinkles, in shadow. A silhouette can also be used to emphasize shape and is very effective if the sun is low enough to give a rim of light round the subject.

COPING WITH BACKLIGHT
When faced with a subject positioned against a large expanse of bright background, you can set the exposure calculated from an overall reading of the scene. This will give you a silhouette image of the subject, and a correctly exposed background. Or, you can calculate the exposure from a close-up reading of the subject. You will then get a correctly exposed subject but an over-exposed background. The final choice is to use a reflector to fill in shadows on the subject (above). Again, take the reading from close to the subject, but as it is now much brighter the exposure will be much more accurate for the whole picture.

45

Low light and fast films

Wide aperture lenses and ultra-fast films extend photography into dim lighting conditions without using flash. Nearly all SLRs have standard lenses with maximum apertures of around f2·8.

ISO 1000 and ISO 1600 colour print and slide films are readily available. Monochrome films with similar speed ratings are made, but they are less easy to track down. Additional speed can be gained from colour slide and monochrome films by adapting the processing.

The main advantage of fast film is that it enables you to use faster shutter speeds in really dim conditions, so avoiding camera shake. Generally, the faster the film, the more expensive it is and the more grainy the result.

By special processing, most colour slide and monochrome films can be pushed so that they give one or two stops more speed. Colour negative film cannot be pushed.

LOW LIGHT LIMITS
SLRs with lenses that have a maximum aperture of f1·8 or f1·4 give good leeway in low light. They also offer greater flexibility in the selection of shutter speeds.

COLOUR BALANCE
Daylight balanced film gives an orange result in artificial light. Tungsten balanced film gives truer results. The fastest tungsten film is ISO 640 and it can be uprated even higher.

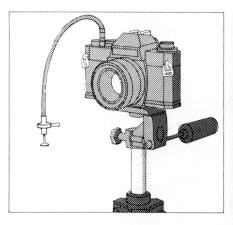

USING A TRIPOD
For perfect sharpness in long exposures – 1/15 and under – use a tripod and a cable release (above). If the exposure time is longer than a second the film may need more exposure than your meter indicates. Add half as much exposure again for times between 1 and 5 seconds, and double the exposure for times from 5 to 20 seconds. When your shot includes a light source, either expose for that, leaving the background dark, or give the shot more exposure to show the rest of the scene.

MOVING LIGHTS
With your camera on a tripod you can record moving lights as streaks of light. Give long enough exposure for the whole movement to be recorded from start to finish.

EXPOSURE
Be careful not to over-expose coloured lights, fires or fireworks because the colour will be lost. Use a smaller aperture (f8 or f11) for exposures of 1/15 or 1/8 on ISO 400.

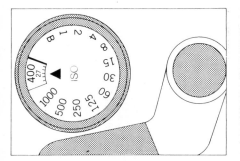

CHOOSING A FAST FILM
Black and white films: fast black and white films tend to give low contrast results. You can easily tailor their processing to cater for under-exposure.
Colour negative films: these have wide exposure latitude and are the most likely to give satisfactory results in difficult lighting conditions. Unlike most colour slide and monochrome films, colour negative film cannot be pushed.
Colour slide films: these need far more exact exposure but give dramatic results when lighting levels are low.
Tungsten balanced films: the speed choice for tungsten balanced films is limited. The fastest ISO 640 film is good for uprating.

CONCERTS AND THEATRE
Faster film makes fast shutter speeds possible in stage lighting. Meter the lit areas with a hand-held meter or go in close for a TTL meter reading and use it for all shots.

OUTDOOR SHOTS
When shooting at dusk or in well-lit night time streets, base your exposure on the subject alone. If the shot includes bright street lights, allow twice the overall TTL meter reading.

UPRATING FILM
If there is not enough light to use even ISO 400 film and you do not want to use a tripod and a slow shutter speed, you can uprate or push your film during processing.
With ISO 400 film, for example, simply set your ISO dial to ISO 800 (one stop faster) or ISO 1600 (two stops faster) and use the TTL meter in the usual way. When the film is finished send it to the processor marked 'Pushed one/two stops'. (You can only deal with complete films in this way, not individual frames.) The special process may cost from 50-100% more than normal: more laboratories offer this service for slides than for print film.

DISADVANTAGES OF UPRATING
When a film is pushed beyond its officially rated speed its properties alter. There are several disadvantages.
The grain: becomes coarser and far more noticeable.
The colours: lose saturation and may tend to shift towards red or green.
The sharpness: is poor compared to normally rated film.
Black or dark parts of the picture: may look grey or slightly coloured, even where there is no discernible shadow detail.
Nevertheless, push processing is a way to get good pictures where it would be impossible to get a picture at all with normally rated film.

EXPOSURE GUIDE

Group 1: very bright subjects, neon signs, shop windows with spotlights
Group 2: bright subjects, fairy lights, festive illuminations, well-lit streets, shop windows, fairgrounds
Group 3: average subjects, floodlit buildings (white light), streets in white (mercury) light)
Group 4: dull subjects, coloured floodlighting, streets in yellow (sodium) light
Group 5: very dull subjects, moonlit landscapes

	ISO 400	ISO 1600
Group 1	1/60 sec at f5·6	1/250 sec at f5·6
Group 2	1/30 sec at f4	1/15 sec at f4
Group 3	½ sec at f5·6	⅛ sec at f5·6
Group 4	5 sec at f8	1¾ sec at f8
Group 5	20 min at f8	5 min at f8

How to use electronic flash

A flashgun will almost certainly be among the first accessories you buy for your SLR camera.

Flash bulbs can only be used once and must then be replaced. Electronic flash will give anything from 50 to several hundred flashes from one set of batteries, depending on its type. It can be connected to the camera either by cable or hot shoe and produces a very short but intense burst of light at the moment the shutter is fully open.

You can use electronic flash whenever the existing light is so dim that you would otherwise have to use very wide apertures – losing depth of field and sharpness – or shutter speeds too slow for hand-held exposures. It is also useful when the subject is unevenly lit or the light, however bright, is coloured. The colour of the light from bulbs and electronic flashguns is matched to colour films to give results similar to sunlight.

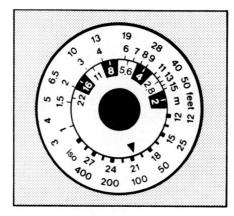

MANUAL FLASH
Simple flash units require manual exposure estimation. Most guns provide a calculator dial for this purpose on the back of the unit. On it you will need to set the film speed. Then you can read off the required aperture setting against the relevant flash to subject distance.

AUTOMATIC FLASH
Automatic flashguns cost more than manual guns but are far easier to use. An auto unit monitors the flash reflected from the subject and cuts off the light as soon as the reflected beam reaches the unit's sensor. The energy-saving circuitry depends on a fast reacting thyristor switch which stops the flash discharge at the moment of correct exposure. With an auto unit you still have to enter the film speed manually.

DEDICATED FLASH
A dedicated flash unit links into the camera's TTL metering to provide fully automatic flash exposures (in some cases even the film speed is set automatically).

EXPOSURE ERRORS
The picture above is the result of a flash exposure error, most likely to happen when you reframe a shot without readjusting the flash. It can be caused by setting the wrong ISO speed on the calculator dial; setting the wrong aperture when using manual flash; or going in too close for the flash range of an automatic gun.

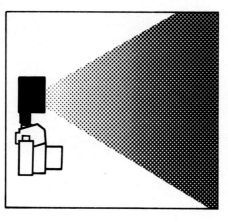

FLASH AND DISTANCE
One of the characteristics of a small light source like flash is that the further away you place a subject the less light it receives. You can see from the diagram above that the light has to cover a greater area the further it travels. In fact, if you double the distance between the flash and the subject, the subject will receive only a quarter of the light, because the area over which the light is distributed is now four times greater than it was originally. This is known as fall off with distance.

AVOIDING FALL OFF
The picture above shows the effect of fall off. As the people get further from the flash they receive less light and so appear darker in the picture.
If you want to avoid this there are two ways you can do so. You can choose an angle from where all of the subject is roughly the same distance from the flash.
Alternatively, you can reduce the relative distance between the different parts of the subject by moving further away and recomposing the shot.

FLASH SYNCHRONIZATION
Because the burst of light from an electronic flash is so brief (1/1000 of a second or faster) you must be sure that at the moment the flash fires the whole of the frame of film is exposed to its light. With most focal plane shutters the whole frame is only exposed at shutter speeds up to 1/60. At faster speeds only part of the frame is exposed at any one moment. (You can see the result in the shot above.) Many SLRs have a flash sync setting on the shutter speed ring in addition to the speed range.

HEAVY FLASH SHADOW
The light from a flashgun is far more concentrated and direct than light from the sun and can cast heavy shadows. This usually happens when the subject is positioned too close to the background (see above). If the flashgun is mounted on top of your camera, and you are standing directly in front of the subject, then the problem may not arise. But if you are using the camera turned vertically the flash will be to one side of the lens and the shadow will be painfully obvious.

LOSING THE SHADOW
To get rid of harsh, unnatural flash shadow, you can move the subject away from the background, as above; use an extension cable for the flash and hold it well above the camera; place the subject against a dark or black background; move the subject into a doorway so that the shadow is lost behind; move the flash, or yourself, far to one side so that the shadow falls outside the frame area or you can stand on a chair and direct the flash towards your subject from above.

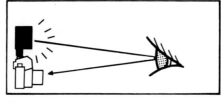

RED EYE
Red eye is a recurrent bugbear in all flash pictures. Sometimes it happens, sometimes it doesn't; some flashguns seem to produce it more often than others.
It often occurs when the subject is staring at the lens, with the pupils of the eyes dilated because of dim natural light. The flash light goes into the eye and reflects off the retina at the back. It will only happen if the flash, eye and lens are aligned and the pupils of the eyes are wide open.

THE WRONG APPROACH
Light is most likely to reflect back from the retina into the lens when you use a small flashgun mounted directly on the hot shoe of your camera close to the lens axis.

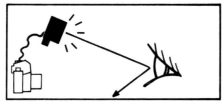

THE CORRECT APPROACH
If you move the flash away from the lens, you change the angle of incidence and reflection. Hold the flash away from the camera by using a cable extension or use a side-mounted flash bracket to avoid red eye.

LOOKING AWAY
Another way to prevent red eye is to tell your subject to look away from the camera. With the subject looking away you can then use your flash mounted directly on to the hot shoe of your camera.

Understanding your flash equipment

Electronic flashguns are easy to use, but it is harder to control their effect. You can see when daylight is unusually bright or dim, or when parts of a picture are unevenly lit. You can also see ugly shadows and poor lighting from the sun. With flash, you cannot assess the lighting before you take the picture. The results can be unpredictable, unless you are sure of your basic flash techniques.

Light from the flashgun falls off rapidly with distance. This happens because it is a small light source used very close to the subject.

If you look at the diagram on the right you will see that when the light from the flashgun has travelled twice the distance it is spread over four times the area. This means that, in practice, whenever you double the distance between the flashgun and the subject, you need to open up the aperture by two stops (or increase the power of the flash accordingly).

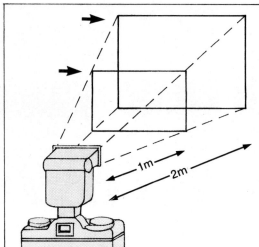

TABLE OF GUIDE NUMBERS
Work out the f stop to use for any distance with your gun's power specification, given as a guide number.
The guide number divided by the distance gives you the f stop for ISO 100 film.

GN	distance	f stop
45	10m	f4·5
45	5-6m	f8
45	4m	f11
16	10m	f1·4
16	5-6m	f2·8
16	4m	f4

MANUAL CALCULATIONS
Manual flashguns put out a constant amount of light and correct exposure is obtained by adjusting the lens aperture depending on different flash to subject distances.
Most units give exposure information relating film speed to these details. The gun slots into the camera hot shoe, the shutter speed control is set to flash, and the lens is manually adjusted to the working aperture for the film in use.

AUTO SETTINGS
Automatic flashguns put out a variable amount of light. You set an aperture on the lens according to the power of the gun. The flashgun (or camera) has a sensor which measures the amount of light which is bounced back from the subject, and cuts off the flash when the subject has been correctly exposed. Automatic flash units compensate for the inverse square law, emitting four times the light for double the distance.

DEDICATED FLASH
Most modern SLR cameras have dedicated flashguns which are intended for use with that make or model only. There are also some flash units which fit a range of cameras by means of adaptors. The basic hot shoe fitting (illustrated above) is not changed, but includes a small second contact and sometimes a third. The extra contact links the flash unit to the camera's exposure and shutter controls.
With most makes, when the flashgun is charged this sets the shutter automatically to the correct speed. It may also trigger a light in the viewfinder.

AUTO SETTINGS
On auto-exposure SLRs, the flashgun may set the lens to the correct f stop as well as setting the shutter speed. But with most makes it simply switches the camera from normal operation to flash, so that there is no chance of your forgetting to change the settings. On some guns the film speed is automatically transferred to the flash unit from the ISO dial. The picture above was taken with a hot-shoe mounted dedicated flash.

OVER-RIDING FLASH
With dedicated flashguns, you can shoot before the flash has recycled. In the gap between taking one picture and the flash ready light coming on for the next, the camera will work just as if no flash were fitted. For the picture above, the camera set an available light exposure as the flash was not ready to fire. This saves wasting a frame, but the colour balance is likely to be wrong (the household lighting has given an orange colour cast). Exposure was 1/30 at f2.

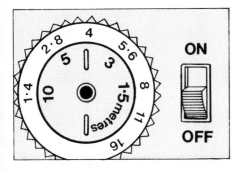

DISTANCE LIMITS

Neither manual nor automatic flashguns will give the correct results unless you keep strictly within fixed distance limits. On a manual gun (shown above) you can see that the greater distances need wider apertures, and shorter ones need smaller apertures. If your lens does not open up or close down to the required aperture, you cannot take your flash picture at that distance. With automatic flashguns, the f stop you set determines the range of working distances. Some automatic guns offer a choice of f stop settings. The wider apertures allow shooting at greater distances.
The limits are usually stated clearly on the gun. If not, refer to your flashgun instruction book.

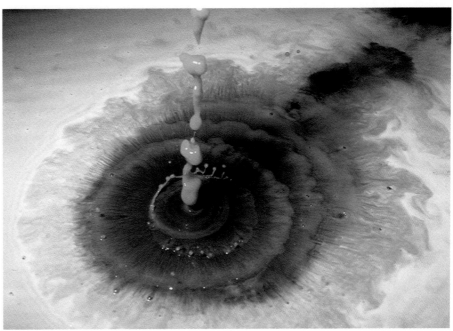

FLASH DURATION

When used very close up, automatic exposure flashguns only emit a short burst of light, lasting as little as 1/30,000 sec, making possible shots like the one above.

THYRISTOR CIRCUITS

All flashguns will take a few seconds to recharge after each shot unless they include a special circuit which uses a thyristor. This saves time by storing unused charge for the next flash.

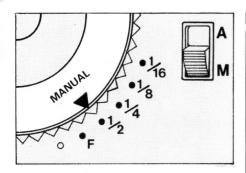

VARIABLE POWER

Some flashguns use the same circuit which controls the automatic exposure to give variable power on manual. A typical power ratio dial is shown in the diagram above.
With the switch set to M (manual) instead of A (auto), you have a choice of full, half, quarter, one eighth and sometimes one-sixteenth power. On some guns, changing this also adjusts the calculator dial. On others you have to make the necessary one, two, three or four stop exposure compensation separately. Autowinder flashguns use this feature to give very short recycling times on low power output.

FILL-IN FLASH – MANUAL

The variable power facility also makes it easier to fill in dark subjects outdoors. If a nearby subject is backlit (as above) and the background is bright, flash brightens up the main subject. Set the shutter speed for flash, and set the aperture that is needed for the background scene. Then set the manual power control on the flashgun to give the light needed for the next widest f stop so that the gun gives out less light for the wider aperture.

FILL-IN FLASH – AUTO

With auto exposure flashguns where there is a choice of aperture, fill-in flash is also quite easy. Set the lens to the aperture one smaller than the aperture required by the flashgun and check that the shutter speed that this aperture gives for the background is not too fast. You will then get fill-in flash automatically (as above). The newest model cameras have sync speeds at 1/250 and the newest flashes use infra red rangefinding or TTL reading for fill-in flash.

Improve your flash technique

The most natural-looking photographs are taken by daylight, whether sunny or overcast. Flash is the simplest alternative to daylight, but the effect is ugly. You need to know a little more than the basic techniques to approach the natural effect of daylight.

Bounce flash is a method of improving the quality of flash light. The light from a flashgun is reflected from a suitable surface on to the subject. The larger the surface, the softer and more diffused the light becomes. The light will still be coming from one direction so larger objects will still form large, soft-edged shadows, but these will be lighter than with direct flash. As on an overcast day outside, small details and projections will cast hardly any shadows at all, giving a far less jagged, angular impression of the picture's subject. It is not a good plan to use bounce flash if the ceiling is dark or high, or if the floor is very dark.

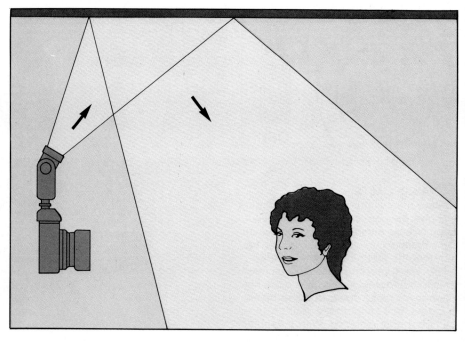

BOUNCE THEORY
For bounce flash to work properly, the reflecting surface must be positioned between the subject and the camera – above, below or to one side of the camera to subject axis.

BUILT-IN BOUNCE
In the diagram above, the flashgun is mounted on the camera but aimed upwards. Flash heads that tilt in this way are a feature of many electronic flashguns.

BOUNCE REFLECTORS
Sometimes a room is too large for the walls or the ceiling to be used as reflectors. In that case, use a portable reflector. Any light surface will do, if it is held at the right distance and angle to the subject. A matt white is best. Some flashguns have a clip to hold a small sheet of white card at 45° to the flash head. Aim the gun up vertically and the card will reflect the light towards the subject.
The shadows will not be as soft as when the light is reflected from a larger surface and the light will come more from the front of the subject than from above.

USING A CARD
A sheet of white card – 20cm × 30cm – was held at 45° on top of the gun. The effect (above) is harsher and more frontal than the ceiling bounce.

COLOUR PROBLEMS
Light bounced from a coloured surface will take on that colour and result in a colour cast like the one in the picture above.

EXPOSURE CALCULATIONS
Camera-to-subject distance governed the exposure for this direct flash shot. Base exposure on flash-to-reflector plus reflector-to-subject distances – plus 1½-2 stops.

AUTO-BOUNCE EXPOSURE
Auto-exposure computer flash needs no extra calculations. Ensure the sensor is pointing at the subject and that the distance the flash travels is within the gun's range for that f stop.

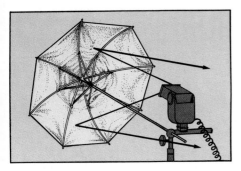

UMBRELLA FLASH REFLECTORS
The best flash light set-up for portraits is to use a flashgun and a reflector on a stand. The easiest reflector to use in this case is an umbrella, shown above. The flash light is aimed directly back into the umbrella, which has a silver or a white surface. The light is bounced back on all sides and the effect is like that of window light. It does produce shadows, but these are soft edged. Because the whole set-up is mobile, you can position the shadows wherever you like. The shot on the right was taken with an umbrella flash, and shows good modelling on the face of the subject.

MODELLING LAMPS
Position a photoflood or domestic light bulb next to the flash shining into the umbrella. This will throw the same shadows as the flash.

TWIN-TUBE FLASH
Bounce flash from a ceiling can give dark eye shadows (top). Twin-tubes have a small second flash which fills in these shadows (bottom).

Flash lighting with a difference

Although direct on-camera flash and bounced flash are useful for photographs which simply take a record of the subject, they are difficult to use creatively.

One fundamental problem with using flash is that you cannot see the effect until the flash is fired. If you have time, you can hold an ordinary desk lamp in the position where the flash will be to see the effect. For more accurate results, you can buy a stand which holds your flashgun next to a reflector light bulb. Studio flash has a modelling lamp built in next to the flash. Coloured filters are available for both studio flash and hand-held flashguns, and these can add life to your pictures. With studio flash, you can control the spread of light with snoots (which cut it down to a spot), barn doors and honeycombs (both make the light more directional). There are diffusers which soften hand-held flash, and lenses which narrow it for use with telephotos.

STUDIO FLASH
Mains studio flash (shown on the left of the picture) gives a full preview of the final lighting effect by using modelling lamp. Light control accessories (in the foreground) include reflectors, diffusers and filter holders. This particular model can also be converted for use with batteries.

RING FLASH
For close-up work, the circular ring flash (shown on the right of the picture) gives completely shadow-free lighting. The model illustrated is low in power and ideal for ISO 100 film. Ring flash is particularly suitable for macro photography of small subjects like plants and insects.

MULTI-FLASH EFFECTS
With most computer flashguns that have energy-saving thyristor circuitry, you can fire a burst of flashes with the shutter open to show a moving subject as a series of frozen, overlapping images in one frame. Any additional light should be dim, and you must be able to fire the flash very quickly. Work close-up, at about 1m, with the widest computer aperture on the gun and the camera set at two stops smaller. Use a tripod and set a shutter speed of one-second. Press out four flashes while the camera makes its exposure. Hold the flash with one hand, and tap the flash button with the other.

THYRISTOR
A thyristor flashgun to get multi-images will work only at close distances when the gun uses so little energy that one basic charge will give five or six quick flashes.

DISCO STROBES
You can get a similar effect by photographing in disco strobe light, as in the picture above. Use a long exposure to catch several images of your moving subject.

COLOURED FLASH

If your subject is netural-coloured, like the stainless steel tumblers above, simply fixing a colour filter to your flashgun can add colour to the picture without changing the subject. Whatever form of flash you are using, you can change the colour of the light it throws: all you have to do is tape some coloured acetate (available in art shops) over the flash head. If you are using more than one flashgun or supplementing daylight, you will add an accent of colour: the overall balance is not upset and the parts lit by coloured flash stand out. Position the flash with the colour filter to one side, not too close to the camera, for best effects.

EXPOSURE AND RESULTS

You need give no extra exposure with light-coloured filter material but with denser filters, it is best to bracket your shots to be safe. If you are using more than one flash, remember that where opposite colours – like red and green or yellow and blue – overlap, a combination close to normal white light will result. In the pictures above, one low-power white flash was aimed from the right, making a strong shadow. A flash twice as strong was aimed from the left at the same distance. This was fitted first with a red, then a blue, a yellow and a green filter in that order. The effect of the colour is best seen in the shadow areas where it is most noticeable.

FILTER KITS

Many battery flashguns which fit into camera hotshoes have special filter kits, like the one above. A kit and two flashguns gives you many effects.

CLOSE-UP FLASH

With extreme close-ups, a hotshoe mounted flash often aims above the subject. The light may also be too directional and concentrated to give good detail. For shallow subjects, where a sharp fall-off does not matter, use a close-up bracket-mounted flash. There are also special filter-rim mounts, and lens-shades with a flash shoe (shown above, top of picture). For deeper subjects use an L-bracket, mounting the flash to the side and allowing angle and pitch adjustment. Ring flash (shown in the foreground) gives superb, shadow-free, consistent lighting from around the lens.

BRACKET FLASH RESULTS

The shot above was taken with the flash fixed at about 15cm above and to the side of the kitten's face. As a result there are strong shadows and a sharp fall-off of light.

RING FLASH RESULTS

The same subject taken with the ring flash is much more detailed and evenly lit, though it has less textural contrast. The same aperture of f16 on ISO 100 film was used.

What filters can do for your pictures

Basic filters are simply flat glass sheets or discs which filter out unwanted wavelengths, or colours of light when fitted to the lens to improve the quality of your pictures.

When used with black and white film, the job of a filter is to improve the tones of a subject. With colour film a filter is used to improve the colour. Use colour filters with discretion when using colour film.

Filters also have an effect on exposure. All but the weakest filters cut down the amount of light entering the lens, and so require increased exposure. The filter factor is usually marked on the rim of each filter. If the filter factor is × 1, then no exposure increase is needed. If it is × 2 then exposure must be increased by one stop (ie, doubled).

You cannot always trust a TTL meter to give correct readings with a strong filter in place. Check by taking a reading without a filter and multiplying this by the marked factor.

FILTERS FOR BLACK AND WHITE
The filters above are most commonly used in black and white photography. They all cut down distant haze and increase contrast, especially between clouds and the sky. From top to bottom they are: UV/haze; X2 yellow; X4 orange; and X8 red.

FILTERS FOR COLOUR
Filters for colour are usually weaker than those used for black and white. They are used to increase the depth of colour and correct unwanted colour casts. Above are: UV/haze (top); skylight 1A (right); polarizer (left); and blue daylight-to-artificial light.

CUTTING THROUGH HAZE
Haze, ultra-violet (UV) and skylight filters all cut down excessive blue from ultra-violet rays for distant subjects and cut through haze on bright overcast days, like that shown above left and none need exposure increases. With the filter fitted the colours become clearer and brighter (above right).

MAKING COLOURS RICHER
A polarizing filter can make a dramatic difference. Skies will appear bluer, grass greener, and the colours will generally look richer. The right-hand side of the picture above was taken with a polarizing filter fitted. A polarizer requires at least 1½ to 2 stops extra exposure.

CUTTING OUT REFLECTIONS
A polarizing filter is also useful for cutting out unwanted reflection from polished, painted or glass surfaces. The right-hand side of the picture above was taken using a polarizing filter. It will also cut glare from water, and works equally well with black and white or with colour film.

56

TO CORRECT TUNGSTEN LIGHT
Colour films are balanced to give correct colours only under one type of lighting. Most are daylight films for normal daylight or flash, but you can buy films balanced for tungsten floodlight bulbs and cine lights. The result of using a daylight film by tungsten light is shown above – an orange cast. The blue D-to-A (daylight-to-artificial) filter shown opposite corrects this. Tungsten balanced film used in daylight does the reverse and gives a strong blue cast, needing an orange-brown A-to-D filter. Both of these filters need exposure increases.

TO CORRECT FLUORESCENT LIGHT
Although fluorescent tube lighting is now very common, no colour films are balanced for this. Tubes vary in colour output, but usually give a greenish cast, as above. Normal daylight film can be partially corrected by using an FL-D (fluorescent-to-daylight) filter, which is warm salmon pink in colour and needs no exposure increase. The correction is never total.
Correction filters are not so essential with colour negative films, as the colour balance can be corrected when printing, but prints will be easier to make and better if you do use one.

CORRECT RENDERING
The picture above was taken on daylight film. The girl was lit by tungsten light. With a blue D-to-A filter fitted to the lens the orange cast, which was so obvious in the first picture, has been greatly reduced. Using a filter will rarely give perfect results, but the effect is much more acceptable.

INCREASING CONTRAST
Black and white film sees colour simply as tones. Blues record as bright and reds as dark. You can use coloured filters to increase contrast. In the pictures above the boots are red, the hat blue, the grass green and the sky pale blue. It was taken without a filter. Compare this with the two on the right.

YELLOW: THE BASIC FILTER
A medium yellow filter will correct a black and white film's over-sensitivity to blue. Apart from improving contrast between the clouds and the sky it cuts down haze and improves foliage and skin tones. The picture above was taken using an X2 yellow filter. Exposure had to be increased by one stop.

RED: FOR DRAMATIC TONES
The deep red X8 filter used for the picture above almost totally cuts out blue light. It also needs a full three stops extra exposure. Contrast is taken to extremes; dark green or blue objects (note the helmet) become almost black. Shadows lose detail and skin is bleached white.

Easy effects with filters

With most special effect filters you need not alter your exposure technique: what you see in the viewfinder represents the finished result but with some filters the degree to which they alter the image depends on the aperture used. So you should use your stop-down preview button to check the final effect before you shoot.

Coloured filters are available in plain tints, with one half only coloured, or with the outer surround coloured and the centre clear. Some are multi-coloured.

Misty filters look slightly opaque and give a pastel or foggy-day effect without making the image unsharp.

Soft-focus filters blur the outline of the image slightly for a diffuse effect.

Screen filters also blur the image and add rainbows or streaks of light. The most dramatic effects with cross-screen filters are produced with strong point-source lamps against a dark background.

MOUNTED FILTERS
Filters mounted in screw-in circular rims (shown in the foreground above) fit only one lens size, though you can buy adaptors. They are expensive, but are of very good optical quality.

SYSTEM FILTERS
Rectangular plastic filters slot into a holder (at the back above) and cost much less. One holder fits several lens sizes and adaptors are cheaper, but the filters are easily damaged.

SPOT FILTERS
Spot or centre-focus filters reinforce the natural emphasis towards the centre of the picture by deliberately misting, blurring or colouring the outside edges. How sharp the central area remains depends on the filter, the lens and which f stop you use. The shot above was taken at f8 with a violet centre-spot filter. Types of spot filter include ones which use a close-up lens with a hole cut in it to blur the outer edges optically; filters with sand-blasted or etched surfaces; coloured glass with a hole cut in the middle; and clear plastic with a pattern printed round the outside.

CROSS-SCREEN FILTERS
Filters with fine parallel lines across the entire surface produce distinctive bursts of light from any bright light sources in the picture. The light bursts follow the direction of the ruled lines, and can be altered by rotating the filter. Here the lines cross at 90°: Rules which cross at 60° produce six-pointed stars. The closer the lines, the stronger the effect. Lines 4mm apart give small light bursts, and lines 1mm apart give strong light bursts. Very fine, closely drawn lines will also cause diffusion, reducing the sharpness and the contrast of a picture to a marked degree.

COLOUR-BURST FILTERS
Ruled with very fine lines, colour-burst filters produce patterns of rainbow colours from strong light sources. There are many variations on this idea, but they are relatively expensive. The stronger the rainbow effect, the more diffusion is produced in the rest of the picture – in some cases as strong as the diffusion from a fog filter. The filter used above has a clear centre spot to reduce this fogging. It throws off repeated parallel images from light sources, in this case extending to the sides of the frame. Rotating the filter changes the angle of the rainbow of light.

COLOUR FILTERS

Straightforward colour filters are ideal for creating a mood, but if you want bright colour effects – strong red or purple for example – you should choose a very graphic, simple image. When shooting in colour, you can make use of filters intended for black and white film, for colour correction, or for darkroom use to give a powerful effect. Normally, you should take your TTL meter reading with the filter in place, but if you want to boost the colour, give the exposure that you would have used if you had been shooting without a filter. But go easy with strong colours: you can always add extra colour at the darkroom stage when you are printing if you decide the print needs a more powerful effect.

MULTI-IMAGE PRISMS

Prisms are thicker than filters – like cut glass with angled facets. They split the subject into overlapping images. There are many types, most of them giving a main image surrounded by slightly weaker secondary ones. The type used above gives a row of repeated images to the left of the frame. Prism filters do not require any change in exposure, but their success depends on the lens and the aperture. They do not work well with telephotos, and at small apertures the image weakens towards the outer edges of the frame. Prismatic filters are most effective with strongly outlined subjects and silhouettes. Unfortunately, prisms tend to be expensive as plastic cannot be used to make most types.

SOFT FOCUS

A soft focus filter gives a basically sharp image surrounded by a diffused halo. Here the pattern on the jumper is sharp, though in the highlight areas the halo is quite strong.

FOG AND PASTEL FILTERS

A fog or pastel filter looks like a clear, colourless filter that has become slightly misted. It diffuses light over all the picture, and has two main uses: Used for portraits, it softens the tones and the colours. Outdoors it gives the impression of a hazy day. Pastel filters are not as strong as fog filters, and both come in two strengths. The picture above was taken with a Pastel 2: more exposure would have given more of an impression of mist, whereas normal exposure simply gives a soft grey effect. Graduated fog filters give a realistic haze to landscape pictures.

GRADUATED FILTERS

Graduated colour filters allow you to colour or darken one half of the picture and leave the rest unchanged. They are usually used to put colour into a plain white sky on a dull day, as above. They can also deepen an already blue sky or add an unexpected green or pink. Grey half-and-half graduated filters are useful if one half of the picture is better lit than another. Indoors, for example, they darken the ceiling and the lights. You can also use two graduated filters together: on a dull day, a brown will warm the ground and a blue will colour the sky.

FILTER TYPES AND FITTINGS

Screw-in mounted filters:
40·5mm, 43·5mm, 46mm, 49mm, 52mm, 55mm, 58mm, 62mm, 67mm, 72mm, 77mm

Filter systems:

Cokin	67×76mm
Ambico	67×76mm
Hoyarex	76×76mm
Kodak	50×50mm
	75×75mm

Filter types:
Pure colour: available in all types. Made in glass, plastic, acetate and gelatin.
Pastel and fog: both rim-mounted and system types.
Graduated: both mounted and system.
Soft focus: mounted filters only.
Centre spot: both rim-mounted and system filters.
Cross screens: both rim-mounted and system filters.
Colour burst: best as permanent, mounted filters.
Prisms: mainly mounted.

Better picture composition

When you look at a scene, your eyes scan everything in front of them rapidly. They take in the important details quickly but catch only a vague idea of the complete scene.

The camera, however, does the opposite. It isolates one part, cuts out all the surroundings, and produces a rectangular picture. The world appears condensed and flattened, into a two-dimensional design in which every visible detail counts.

Because of this, careful composition is essential. Better composition leads to better pictures. Accidental framing of the wrong area, can ruin an otherwise good picture.

The golden rule is: Don't aim – frame.

Frame up your shot using the edges of the viewfinder, don't aim just using the centre. You will then avoid cut off detail, bad positioning and crooked horizons.

FRAMING FOR SLIDES
The whole area of a 35mm frame is rarely seen. The SLR viewfinder only shows 93% of the area (the solid line above) and mounts for slides cover up about the same amount.

FRAMING FOR PRINTS
If your prints are made commercially you are likely to see even less of the frame area. Most firms crop the edges as far in as the dotted line shown above so leave a little extra space at the edges.

BALANCE
Balance is one of the most important aspects of composition. It takes a while to learn and involves a certain amount of instinct. But there are a few basics which can be grasped quite easily. The first thing to look out for is the horizon. If this is not level then the components of the picture will seem to tumble out (see above). It is easy to forget about the horizon if your main subject is in the foreground or middle distance, so remember to check it carefully in the viewfinder.

BALANCING VERTICALS
If you aim your camera upwards at a building, as above, the sides are bound to appear to converge. This can be effective if balance is achieved by aligning the verticals so that they lean equally on either side. The shot above left, shows an attempt to keep the building straight by making one side roughly parallel with the edge of the frame. It fails – the horizon slopes and, despite being lined up with vertical, the building looks as if it is about to topple over.

BALANCING MASSES
You can reduce the leaning of a building by photographing it from a distance but the chances are that it will then fill only a small part of the frame, leaving large empty spaces. When this happens change your viewpoint slightly. Crouch down or move to the side so that you can include another element in the picture to balance the main subject in the distance. In the picture above a change of viewpoint has included the bushes and flowers in the foreground to counter-balance the building.

60

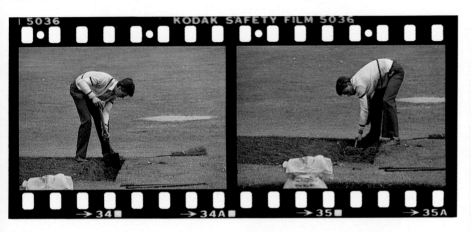

READING THE PICTURE

The eye doesn't see all of a picture at once. It wanders over it, picking out details and returning to the most interesting parts. Good composition helps the eye by linking and balancing the different parts of the picture. Good pictures hold the eye so that the viewer returns repeatedly to the important details. Choose a viewpoint that emphasizes the main subject and excludes distracting details or colour from the background and edges of the picture area.

POSITIONING THE SUBJECT

Look at the two pictures of the man digging above. In the left-hand shot, the man is facing the right, and the action aims right.

Right-facing subjects seem to look out of the picture. Left-facing subjects stop the eye and hold it better. The picture above looks more contained and the empty spaces are less noticeable. Try to position your subject so that it holds the rest of the picture together. Avoid putting people at the edge of the frame looking away from the subject.

VERTICAL COMPOSITION

Remember that you can turn your camera on its side to take pictures. The same rules of composition apply, only this time to a longer, narrower format suitable for shots like the one above.

COMPOSING FOR IMPACT

Having said that you must keep the horizon level for balanced composition, there are exceptions – especially if the horizon is not actually included in the picture. A tilt can be very effective if it looks deliberate.

In this picture the horizon was certainly not kept straight, but the impression is one of the strength and movement – even though the car was in fact stationary.

By breaking the rules like this, you can often produce a dynamic picture. But make sure the effect is exaggerated.

THE CLASSIC APPROACH

If you are in any doubt about how to compose your picture, you can always fall back on the traditional rule of thirds. Painters have used this system throughout the ages and the result is usually restful and easy to look at. When the main points of interest are on, or near, the intersection of thirds they tend to attract most interest, but without dominating the whole of the photograph.

The picture above is a perfect example of classic composition. The horizon is one third of the distance from the top of the frame, and it is level. The tree is one third of the way in from the right-hand edge, and the mass of yellow in the foreground balances these two centres of interest.

Seeing in colour

The best colour photographs make their impact by means of colour – as well as by good composition, lighting and technical quality.

Colour has a strong effect on our emotions. Different colours can subconsciously suggest many different things. Blue, for example, is associated with coldness, distance, cleanliness, purity and the spirit. Very dark blue has deep and mysterious overtones. This may be because the sky is blue. Brown, the colour of the earth, gives a warm, reassuring, solid, natural impression. Red is dramatic and suggests heat.

You can use colours to the same effect in your photographs. Choose an appropriate colour background for a portrait, for example: use a colour filter for atmosphere: or just learn to see good colour pictures. Study classical paintings to see how colour harmony and contrast can be used; and then develop your own ideas from there.

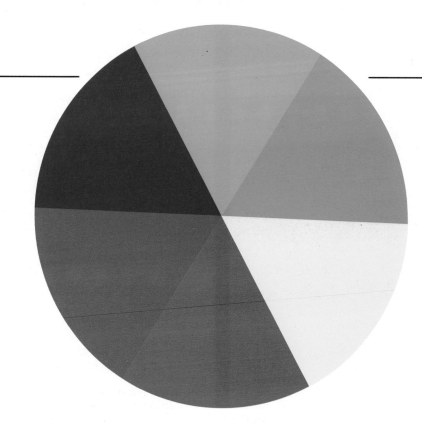

THE COLOUR WHEEL
The colours of the colour wheel are red, yellow, green, cyan, blue and magenta. The primary colours are red, green and blue. The others are complementary colours.

HARMONY AND CONTRAST
Adjacent colours go well together; opposite colours have most contrast. Mixtures of two adjacent colours will clash with the mixture of the two opposite colours.

COLOUR AS THE SUBJECT
A mixture of bright colours makes a good composition with colour as the main interest as in the photograph above. With so many shades, colour clashes are minimized.

COLOUR HARMONY
Pictures in which all the colours harmonize are restful to look at – subtle rather than brash. In this shot the background provides just enough contrast for the subject to stand out.

COLOUR CONTRAST
You can add depth, dimension and brilliance by putting a brightly coloured object, like this orange flower, against a background of its opposing colour on the colour wheel.

HOW COLOURS WORK

Compare the black and white picture above with the colour version of the same subject. The black and white picture is rather pointless, but the identical shot in colour makes a strong impact simply because of the colour. To get the strongest possible effect from the colours in a scene, use slow, fine grain colour film. With colour transparencies, you can get more saturated colour by slightly under-exposing the shot. With colour negatives, you will often get better results from slightly over-exposing the picture. In either case half a stop is normally enough to increase the colour saturation.

COLOUR BLENDS

The saturation of colours is affected by the amount of white they contain. The colours in the picture above are complex blends of hues from the colour wheel mixed with white.

FILM AND PRINTS VARY

On different film, these colours would record slightly differently. To see the bias of a film, photograph a colour checker on one frame and compare the shot with the original.

ONE-COLOUR IMPACT

A shot which uses only one colour can be very powerful, so long as it contains an area of some neutral shade. The slight variations in shades of red maintain the interest.

ACCENT COLOUR

A small area of one colour on a contrasting or neutral background attracts attention. The red button dominates the rest of the picture, despite its small area.

DISCORDANT COLOURS

The colours above are neither in direct contrast nor in harmony. Orange is a mixture of red and yellow: yellow is next to green on the colour wheel and red is next to purple.

Composing for depth

One of the most common reasons for taking a photograph is to record a scene or an event exactly as it appeared at the time.

A photograph, however, does have one major drawback. Because it is only two-dimensional, it is not always easy to convey the feeling of solidness and depth that existed in the original subject. (Many people are disappointed with their pictures because they look flat and not quite true to life, rather like stage scenery.)

This need not happen. With a little thought and care you can bring out the feeling of depth in a subject, so that the size, shape, scale and position of everything in the picture stands out well and clearly. The way to do this is by careful composition. You can change your viewpoint, and maybe even your lens, so that what you include in the frame gives clues about the subject and turns a flat piece of paper into a three-dimensional image.

VIEWPOINT AND DEPTH
Depth in a picture is increased if you shoot at an angle to the subject and not flat-on. Top: 3-D effect, using a low viewpoint and looking into the depth of the scene. Above: flat 2-D with little depth from a straight-on viewpoint.

LENSES AND DEPTH
It is easier to create impressions of depth with a wide angle lens rather than a telephoto. Top: a 200mm lens compresses distance and conveys little depth. Above: a wide angle 24mm, exaggerates depth.

3-D CLUES – SCALE
Use the clues your eyes use to show depth in photographs. The main one is perspective. Things look smaller when they are far away than they do if they are close up. In the shot above, this is the main clue to the depth of the subject. To emphasize this you can move closer to part of the scene, so that objects nearer the camera look even larger. A wide angle lens lets you get closer and still get the whole subject in the frame. The strongest sense of distance is given when there are similar sized objects both near to the camera and in the distance, or a line of them is repeated.

OVERLAP
Distant subjects do not have much depth visually. All the details are so far away that any difference in relative scale is lost. A person 15 metres away, for example, looks five times smaller than a person 3 metres away. But someone 30 metres away only looks half the size of the one 15 metres away. Overlapping detail, as in the shot above, is a much better clue to depth in distant subjects and telephoto lens shots. If one part of the picture overlaps another we know it must be in front of it. Change your viewpoint so that some of the elements in the picture overlap.

FRAMING THE SUBJECT
A frame round the subject gives an even greater impression of depth than the inclusion of a foreground. In this shot, the archway frame adds depth.

SUBJECT WITHOUT DEPTH
The shape of the monument above is clear enough, but seen in isolation the whole picture is flat. There is no interesting distance in the shot. Pictures like this are simple, clear and easy to understand, even if they are small. (For this reason catalogue publishers often cut a subject out of its backgound.) But from this picture you have no idea of the size of the subject. Only the limited depth of the subject itself gives any 3-D effect, and even that would be lost in dull lighting.

USING A BACKGROUND
By standing back and choosing a higher viewpoint, the picture is made much more interesting. A complete background scene now puts the subject in context, and gives it scale. There is much more to look at in the picture, and the impression of three-dimensional depth is increased. Empty space has been filled by scenery, but the main subject is still prominent. Good backgrounds have this effect. A badly-chosen background might have too much distracting detail.

ADDING A FOREGROUND
To complete a scene like this, depth can be emphasized by using a foreground. Sometimes this is impossible, but by looking around you may find a suitable viewpoint to line up foreground, subject and background perfectly. For the picture above, the lens was changed to keep the subject large enough from further away. When you include a foreground, make sure it does not dominate. Sometimes it is enough just to include some space in front of the subject.

CONTRASTING TONES
By making the subject stand out against the dark background of the interior, this 100mm telephoto shot has depth despite very few other 3-D clues.

DOMINANT COLOURS
As well as light and shade, colours can play a part in the impression of depth in a photograph. As a general rule bright and vivid colours look close and larger, while subdued colours look further away and smaller. Warm colours – red, yellow and orange – are the most dominant. They seem to advance out of a picture. Bright purples can also stand out. Because of this property you can use warm, bright colours to add life to a flat picture.

RECEDING COLOURS
To stand out at all, the colder colours – blue and green – have to be really brilliant. Normal blues and greens look further away, smaller and less dominant. Even the bluest sky never seems to dominate, whereas an area of red in a fairly small part of the frame can take over completely. Compare the effect of the two shots above. The flowers take up just about the same area in each picture but the red appears much more lively.

How to use selective focusing

Selective focusing is a way to emphasize the most important part of a picture by making it much sharper than the rest.

The idea is to allow only enough depth of field to cover details you want, leaving the rest a blur. The 35mm SLR is the ideal camera for this: the wide apertures available on many lenses limit depth of field, and the camera's fast shutter speeds allow you to use wide apertures even in good light.

Long lenses are helpful since they have a shallow depth of field, and working close to your subject also limits the area in sharp focus.

An SLR with a depth of field stopdown preview control is an advantage, since it allows you to see precisely what effect your aperture has on the depth of field before you take the picture. However, practice soon allows you to judge depth of field and anticipate the visual effect of various apertures.

ISOLATING WITH BLUR
When a picture contains a great deal of highly colourful or very detailed distractions, use selective focusing to blur them. This is particularly useful in drawing attention to someone's face.

WHERE TO FOCUS
The sharpest focus should be on the most important area of detail: it should preferably contain sharp tones and shapes. In pictures of faces use the eyelashes of the eye nearest to you.

MAKING THE FOREGROUND COMPLETELY DISAPPEAR

There are times when there is no way round an obstructing fence or barrier between you and the subject. By throwing it out-of-focus, however, you may be able to make it seem to disappear in your shot. Your aim is to blur the wire or fence so completely that it is barely visible in the final picture. Get very close to the fence so that it is out of focus. A wide aperture and a telephoto lens (which both limit the depth of field) will be a help here to achieve this.

The first of these shots (above) made no attempt to lose the fence. It was taken at a distance of one metre from the fence at f16 – a typical sunny day aperture.

This shot was taken with the lens right up against the fence at an aperture of f3·5 – which required a 1/1000 sec shutter speed. You can no longer see the fence. It is too out of focus to register on the film. The technique can be very useful when you are photographing at a zoo, for instance, or for some forms of sport where the arena is surrounded by a protective fence. It can also be used to minimize the effect of dust and scratches when you are photographing through the window of a vehicle. When photographing wildlife from a hide, you may also be able to lose the twigs and foliage close to the camera. Remember to focus carefully on the main subject.

A PROBLEM BACKGROUND
Backgrounds can be a problem, particularly in candid shots of people and animals. When you can neither pose the subject against a more suitable background nor change your viewpoint, selective focusing can solve the problem by blurring the background detail. In the first of these shots (above), the red boots distract the eye away from the kitten.

Since getting an animal to pose for the camera is even more difficult than posing people, it was too risky to move the kitten to another location. Nor was it possible to lose the boots by taking another camera angle and still keep the head-on viewpoint.

GET THE RIGHT LIMITS
When you use selective focus, make sure that the main subject is sharp all over. Use the depth of field preview button to check this, or work it out on the depth of field scale if you have no preview button. It is better to allow too much depth of field than cut it short by using too wide an aperture. Remember the rule of thumb that the point you use to focus on in the viewfinder is about one third of the way into the area of sharp focus – not in the middle.

KEEP THE SUBJECT FLAT
When the aperture cannot provide enough depth of field to cover the whole subject, try moving the subject or changing the camera angle. In the shot above, the first picture has the subject at an oblique angle to the camera. Keeping the background blurred also means there is not enough depth of field to keep the whole subject sharp. The second picture (above) shows an alternative composition with the subject flat-on to the camera.

PRE-FOCUSING
When using a telephoto lens and a tripod for wildlife put out suitable bait and focus on that. The subject's head will come into focus when it feeds.

MAKING IT DISAPPEAR
The alternative was to limit the depth of field and leave the boots out-of-focus. Though they are still as brightly coloured, without sharp detail, the blurred outline attracts less attention. The shallow depth of field also means that some of the kitten's body is also slightly out-of-focus though the face itself is sharp. In this case however the slight blur helps to show the kitten's fluffy coat. If you were photographing animals at a zoo, you could use selective focusing to turn an obviously man-made background into a neutral blur. At home by limiting your depth of field you can lose detail on patterned wallpaper to give an even-toned background.

CHANGING THE EMPHASIS OF THE PICTURE
Sometimes the subject of your shot may not be immediately obvious. It could be that the colours of the subject are similar to the background, in which case selective focus may be the only way to pick it out. Or – as in the two pictures above – there could be more than one possible subject for the photograph. Rather than allowing the viewer's attention to wander between one area of the frame and the other, it is better to restrict your depth of field with a wide aperture so that you only have one area completely in focus. In the first shot (above), the poppies are very definitely the main subject, and the background has been left an out-of-focus blur.

In this picture the aperture remained the same but the focus was shifted to the distant buildings. Here the poppies contribute only foreground colour to the distant scene. The effect is quite similar to the effect of focusing with our own eyes: try looking at an expansive view and you will realise that it is impossible to keep the foreground and background in focus at the same time. Switch attention from one object to another and the focus will automatically change to accommodate the new subject. We choose what is the most interesting part of the scene and focus our eyes accordingly. By limiting your depth of field, you can achieve the same effect.

67

The effect of changing viewpoint

Your viewpoint changes the shape and size of your subject. In everyday life we are not normally aware of the way things appear to change shape as we move around them because our brain interprets what our eyes see. If you deliberately look at something familiar from an unaccustomed viewpoint, however, you can become aware of the effect.

The camera never adjusts. Move viewpoint or angle, and shapes of the objects in the viewfinder change radically. Rectangles become trapeziums, circles become ovals, small objects look larger than big ones, fat faces look thin, high foreheads look low. When you change lenses and move closer to keep it the same size in the frame, you change your viewpoint even more dramatically. The brain tries to interpret visual images but it cannot do this well in pictures, so use this effect to your advantage to produce some dramatic photographs.

DISTANCE AND ANGLES
The difference in the effect you get when you change the angle from which you view the subject depends on how far away it is. If you are very close with a wide angle lens there is a very striking difference. In the top strip of pictures – taken on a 24mm lens – the first picture was taken with the photographer kneeling and the subject standing. In the second strip, the positions were reversed.

DISTANCE AND PERSPECTIVE
For the bottom strip of pictures the poses were the same, but because the photographer used a 100mm lens he was working further from the subjects. The difference in viewpoint is far less marked in the first two pictures by comparison with the pair above them. Again, the subjects did not move in the third pictures (top and bottom), yet the perspective has changed with the lens used.

SHAPE AND PERSPECTIVE
Your choice of lens appears to affect the shape of the objects you photograph. This is not due to distortion: it happens because the shorter the lens you use the nearer you have to come to fill the frame with the subject and this distance affects perspective. In the picture above, perspective is exaggerated because it was taken at close quarters with a wide angle lens. The parallel sides of the van are steeply angled and the cab looks unnaturally large by comparison with the rest of the vehicle.

CHOOSING YOUR LENS
In this picture the van looks far more natural, closer to the way we would see it with our eyes. This shot was taken with a 50mm lens from farther away than the first picture. But which effect do you prefer? The picture above gives a more accurate representation but some photographers might prefer to use the wide angle lens. The rather unnatural, exaggerated perspective serves better to catch the viewer's attention simply because it is not the way we would see it.

STEEP PERSPECTIVE OR FLAT?
This shot was taken from even further away using a 100mm lens. By comparison this one makes the van look quite flat, so the relative dimensions are almost true to life. To demonstrate the change of perspective in all three shots, imagine that the lines along the top and bottom of the van extended out of the frame. In the wide angle shot the lines would come together quite quickly, giving a very steep, dynamic perspective. In the 100mm picture the perspective is far gentler.

CONVERGING VERTICALS
Distant objects appear in a photograph on a smaller scale than objects closer to the camera.

If the subject of a photograph includes parallel lines, they will appear to narrow as they get further away and the scale diminishes. When the subject is horizontal, like a road, the effect would be called good perspective. When it is vertical, like the building above, it has a slightly dizzying effect and is called converging verticals. Tilting the camera in relation to the building will exaggerate the effect. A shorter focal length lens will too because it can include more of the foreground which contrasts more strongly in scale to the distant parts.

KEEPING VERTICALS STRAIGHT
Converging verticals are most disconcerting when the sides of the building are only slightly angled by comparison with the sides of the frame. This gives the impression that the building is actually leaning backwards. To counteract this, try to make the building's walls line up with the sides of the viewfinder. The picture above was taken from halfway up a nearby building so that the camera could be kept parallel with the building and still include some of its height. If you cannot find a viewpoint from which you can keep the verticals straight, go in closer and tilt the camera sharply up to exaggerate the effect.

DIVERGENCE
The principle that makes vertical lines appear to converge towards the top of a picture when the camera is angled upwards does the same towards the bottom of the picture when it is angled down. This effect is called diverging verticals, and if it is very marked it can give an impression of vertigo (as in the picture above). If you are photographing from eye level in a small room you may unintentionally cause this effect in a picture, particularly with a wide angle lens and with walls and furniture close by. In a full length portrait, the result might be a big head and small feet: to avoid the problem, shoot from waist level.

FIND A BETTER VIEWPOINT
The sculpture and the building in the picture above make an interesting subject, but are not shown at their best. The subject lacks colour and the lighting is rather dull, so all the more care has to be taken with the composition. Since the subject cannot be moved the alternative is to change the camera position. The eye level position here includes a prominent notice, an unsightly road, unwanted buildings and various other debris. All this detracts from the main subject.

MOVE THE CAMERA
By taking up a kneeling position, moving the camera less than one metre, the composition is improved. The subject stands out and the other distractions are eliminated.

USEFUL ACCESSORIES
A zoom lens – particularly a wide ranging zoom – allows you to change the distance and viewpoint and still fill the frame with the subject. A tripod with a geared central column will also help.

Photographing people

A photograph with someone in it is almost always more compelling than the same shot without the human interest but people are also difficult to photograph well. Apart from the technical and artistic considerations, the photographer has to be conscious of actions, gestures and expressions. And often the presence of the camera itself can have a disastrous effect on these. Sometimes the solution is to ask for co-operation and pose your subject: other times it is better to remain as inconspicuous as possible so that the subject behaves naturally.

Photographers who take pictures of people all the time – like wedding or news photographers – often develop a line of patter that works well for them. There may be no need to go to this extreme, but it is worth thinking about.

Sometimes, if people are tense, you can take a picture and then, unnoticed, take a second picture once they have relaxed.

POSING FOR PICTURES
People seldom act naturally in front of the camera. Often they stiffen up and the pose becomes rather wooden. Help your subject to relax by giving him something to do.

GROUPING PEOPLE
Avoid straight lines in group shots. Get people to stand at different angles and on different levels as above, or ask some of them to sit or kneel, so that you can see all the faces.

EXPRESSIONS AND GESTURES
Expressions and gestures tell us more about the subject of a photograph than anything else. Even if he is obviously badly treated and hungry, a laughing child provokes a smile from the viewer, whereas a sad expression produces a sympathetic sadness in the viewer. Look for familiar expressions for your portraits: shrugs, winks, anger, tears, thumbs-up, fist clenching and so on. These gestures are an instant visual language.

SITUATION INTEREST
Though shots which isolate a figure or face prominently have great impact, the subject's background or environment can add extra interest and information about the subject. When using a background in this way, try to exclude details that are not relevant to the subject. Make sure that the subject is not overwhelmed by the background: a wide angle lens will make your subject appear larger by comparison with the background.

INTERACTION
Wherever two or more people are talking, arguing, haggling, joking or working together, there are opportunities for good pictures. Couples make appealing shots: so do mothers and babies, teachers and children or teams of people working or playing a sport. Look out especially for contact between the subjects – either eye-contact or physical contact, like a protective hand on the arm or a handshake.

PEOPLE AND PLACES
Many pictures of people are taken on holiday or during an outing. To show people against a relevant background, use a standard or a wide angle lens and move far enough back to get the whole building (or mountain, or lake) in the frame. Ask your subjects to come fairly close to the camera and compose the picture so that the group forms a foreground interest without obscuring the background. If you can find a slightly elevated camera position, this will be far easier to do. The picture above shows the right balance between the subjects and the place they were visiting, so that both claim an equal share of the viewer's attention.

TO POSE OR NOT TO POSE?
In answer to this question, first decide why you want to take the picture. If you are taking a picture to remember someone by – someone you may have met briefly on holiday, for example – then you will want a good, clear picture and it would be worth asking the subject to pose against a well-chosen background. Pictures of the family, on the other hand, can be very tedious if they are a succession of formal poses in front of places of interest. Candid pictures taken of events as they happen are far more lively, and you are more likely to get unself-conscious shots when you know the subjects well. This shot was taken on the spur of the moment.

THE RIGHT APPROACH
Never try to pretend that you are not taking a picture of someone when it is clear that you are: this only creates tension and even hostility. Most people will agree to have their picture taken. But they are likely to become rather self-conscious and you may need to direct them. The picture above is spoiled by the fact that the subject is looking rather aimlessly out of the picture so that the interest follows her eyes, out of the picture.

EYE CONTACT
A picture gains immediate impact if the subject is caught looking directly at the camera. Only attract attention when the shot is framed and focused. A name or a funny comment should draw an immediate response and a natural expression. If your finger is on the shutter release, the picture will be there for the shooting. The moment will soon be over – a successful result comes from quick reactions and fast shooting, hence the need for preparation.

CANDID CONCENTRATION
An alternative to direct eye contact is for the subject to concentrate on something within the picture area. Your subject might find this easier to do, and the viewer can follow the attention to another part of the picture. The picture above clearly demonstrates this link, and though the subject obviously knew she was being photographed it is a candid picture because you still get the impression that you are observing her unnoticed.

Portraits of people

A portrait portrays the subject: it may show only what the subject looks like – as in a passport photograph – or it may include details that can sum up their character, lifestyle or occupation, or even their environment. The composition, pose and content of a formal portrait are all well-established: the choice is between head-and-shoulders, full-length or perhaps seated, three-quarter length poses.

Informal portraits are often taken at the subject's home, using natural light with the subject in any normal, relaxed pose. With pictures like this, the intention should be to show the subject as he usually looks rather than how he would like to look for a formal portrait.

Environmental portraits should have a background chosen to inform the viewer about the subject. You might photograph a mechanic at his workshop, or a keen gardener against his flowers.

USING THE SURROUNDINGS
Using both foreground and background as a frame, the picture above shows a couple at work, the composition makes them stand out.

DOUBLE PORTRAITS
A double portrait where a close relationship or teamwork are involved works best if the subjects are close together at the centre of the frame.

HEAD-AND-SHOULDERS PORTRAITS
A picture with both head and torso turned directly towards the camera tends to look like a passport photograph. Allow your subject to relax in a chair, perhaps resting their elbows on a table, and give a few simple directions. Say 'Look over there' to get them to turn their head, and then 'Without moving your head, turn your eyes back to me' to restore eye contact. (If you just say 'Now look at me' they will probably turn the whole head back.)

TIPS ON POSING
The picture above looks far more natural and relaxed than the one on the left. Firstly, the subject is seated sideways on to the camera, which slims the body. Secondly, the head is turned back to face the camera, but not so far that both ears are included. Thirdly, the subject was asked to lean slightly forward to give her head and face a slight angle. You may not want to follow this formula exactly, but think of ways to vary the direct, head-on position.

FULL LENGTH POSES
Avoid straight standing poses: these do not fit the 35mm picture shape. Leaning with the weight mainly on one leg looks better, or seated poses. Try the legs crossed, arms folded, or one hand in a pocket.

EYES ARE CRUCIAL
In any portrait the eyes are the most important detail. You should focus on the eyes and ask your subject to look directly at the camera. Try to avoid heavy shadows under the eyes (as in the picture above). Outdoors, these are just as likely on overcast days as in bright sunshine, so make sure your subject is not inclining the face downwards. Avoid squinting by shooting into the light when the sun is strong. Indoors, arrange your lighting with these points in mind.

CATCHLIGHTS AND REFLECTORS
Catchlights are small pinpoints of light in the pupil (as above) which add sparkle to a portrait. Indoors, a window facing the subject supplies them, but take care: more than one catchlight looks odd. Even in backlighting you can add catchlights by using a flashgun to balance your other lighting and fill in shadows.
Another way to fill in shadows is to use white card or a sheet to reflect the main light back on to the subject.

INCLUDING THE HANDS
Like eyes, hands are also very expressive in a portrait. However, they often look ugly if they are posed badly or too close to the camera. Avoid tight fists or widely spread fingers.

CAMERA ANGLES
Most portraits are taken full-face or threequarter profile, with the camera level with the face. Move the camera for more arresting shots. Profiles like this need less careful lighting and also work well in silhouette.

LOW VIEWPOINTS
A low viewpoint will make a weak chin look stronger and make the nose seem broader but shorter. It will also emphasize the eyes and the whole face will seem more rectangular. But take care with the gaping nostrils.

HIGH VIEWPOINTS
A high viewpoint reduces the size of the chin and emphasizes the hair and the forehead. It tends to slim a wide nose and makes the eyebrows stronger though the eyes may be shaded. It also makes the face look rather triangular.

73

Taking better candid shots

Any picture of people which is not posed and where the subject is not aware of the camera is a candid shot. People photographed candidly are usually more interesting because they are not self-conscious. Curiously, however, the best candid shots are as popular with the subjects themselves as with other viewers. They are often very sympathetic, or humorous, and they reveal character.

Few people really object to being photographed, and some positively expect it, which can be counterproductive for the candid photographer. Take your candid shots quickly and with no fuss. Tourist areas, where people expect to see a number of cameras not necessarily pointing at them, make the best locations for candid shots of strangers. One good plan is to show interest in something near your real subject and pretend to be photographing that.

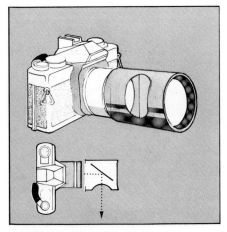

MIRROR ATTACHMENTS
The right angle mirror attachment is specially designed for taking candid pictures without being observed. It will fit most lenses of focal lengths from 50mm to 200mm. It is made to look like a lens hood or part of a longer lens – except for a large round hole in the side. A mirror at 45° to the camera turns the image received through this hole by 90° so that you can shoot at leisure, aiming the camera away from your actual target at right angles. But the picture you see is reversed.

WAIST-LEVEL VIEWS
Some SLRs have interchangeable viewfinders, and to these you can fit a waist-level viewing screen. It gives a picture clear enough to be viewed from above, with the camera held casually, using the focusing scale on the lens. Viewfinder attachments turn the image through 90° so that you can view it from above.

HOME GROUND
Candid pictures are easier when your presence with a camera is accepted – with friends or at home. Carry your camera regularly and people will forget that you have it.

CHILDREN
Small children – especially toddlers tend to play up to the camera. Treat your own children like strangers and shoot your best pictures when they are completely unaware.

CHOICE OF LENSES
Standard lenses have wide apertures which allow you to photograph in dim light without startling flash.
Wide angles allow you to get close to the subject and keep him in focus. They also take in people at the edge of the frame who do not suspect they are included in the picture.
Telephotos cover a very selective area and you may find you have to keep your eye to the viewfinder to judge what is in the frame. But they do allow you to keep your distance.
Zooms are very useful since they allow you to alter the size of your subject without attracting attention by moving around.

MISLEADING AIMING
One way to work openly while leaving your subject unaware that he is being photographed is to aim deliberately wide. Let it appear that you are photographing something beyond your real target. Do not look directly at your subject (except when you have the camera to your eye). Aiming at your mythical subject, include part of your real subject at the edge of your viewfinder (as in the picture above). Make sure that this focusing detail is in the same plane as the face of the subject and that the depth of field is sufficient to cover the important areas. You can take your time over this as long as the subject does not begin to suspect.

. . .AND REFRAMING
Then swing your camera gently round to recompose your shot to include the whole of your real subject (as in the picture above). Even if the subject has noticed you to begin with, by this time he should have lost interest in the camera. If you want more shots of the same subject, return to your decoy subject once more to adjust the camera controls, perhaps taking some shots to complete the illusion. If you are found out, a direct, confronting expression can add impact to your picture. Even though the subject is now aware of you, make sure he has no time to rearrange his expression. Shoot immediately, then shoot again to catch their reaction.

GETTING TOO CLOSE
Few people believe that you can take their picture from less than one metre. With a 24mm or wider lens you can include people who think you are shooting right past them.

TELEPHOTO TECHNIQUE
A long telephoto, like a 500mm lens, is inconvenient to carry about, particularly if you are trying to be unobtrusive in a crowd. It does have its uses for candid photography, however, though it calls for a different approach. Find a suitable vantage point in an inconspicuous place and set the camera up on a tripod in advance.
Focus the lens and wait for the shots you want to materialize. One advantage of using a lens as long as the one used for the picture above is its shallow depth of field. This means that you can isolate the subject clearly against a confused or irrelevant background by differential focusing.

PORTRAIT LENSES
Short telephotos are ideal for pictures of people. They are as convenient to use as a standard with a shallower depth of field and a closer, more intimate view of the subject than he suspects.

BLACK AND WHITE BENEFITS
Candid shots in black and white tend to look more newsy and immediate. There is no colour to distract from expressions. It is also easier to crop and blow up the best details.

Taking better landscape pictures

You can go hunting for good landscape pictures in most parts of the country at any time of the year. Scenic views taken in bright sunshine, autumn colours, delicate spring foliage, frosty branches, mist or snow make fine landscapes.

To be a good landscape photographer you must be prepared to work – in all weathers. If you do catch sight of an exceptional view, the chances are that by walking a few hundred metres you can improve on it enormously.

Pack just the camera gear you need and use your feet. A tripod is cumbersome, but it is a help if you want to ensure sharp pictures with the maximum depth of field. A range of filters will vary the effects you can get – graduated filters to darken the sky, or filters that intensify the colours of the landscape. You should also take plenty of film, but there is no need to weigh yourself down with equipment.

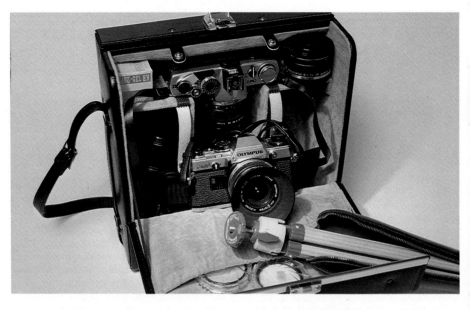

EQUIPMENT TO TAKE
A light tripod with spiked feet is useful as it lets you use long exposures. A 50mm lens, a wide angle and a telephoto zoom are ideal lenses, and a teleconverter may be useful. Take a light camera holdall which you can open and use while it is still slung on your shoulder.

CASES AND BAGS
If you find a holdall too bulky, use separate camera and lens cases with neckstraps. The ever-ready type of case protects the camera against knocks it may get while you are climbing or walking. You can wear one lens slung (bandolier style) over each shoulder.

PROBLEMS WITH LONG EXPOSURES
Slow, fine grain films give landscapes an extra quality. They also require good depth of field and small apertures, so you may well need to use long exposures. Landscapes may look still, but there is always some movement. Water in streams, grass, trees or even clouds blown by the wind: all these make long exposures tricky. On ISO 25 film at f22 and with a polarizing filter, you may need a shutter speed of ½ sec, even on a sunny day. This is long enough for a slight breeze to blur foreground foliage or grass. Try to use this creatively, allowing the water or the rippling grass to make fluid patterns across the frame.

FILTERS FOR HAZE AND UV LIGHT
The distances involved in landscape pictures lead to the problem of haze, which obscures the view progressively into the distance. If the scene looks hazy to the eye, then it will look hazier in the photograph. Even scenes that look clear may seem hazy and rather blue in a picture, because film is more sensitive to blue and ultra-violet (UV) light than the eye is. It is therefore vital to use a haze-cutting filter – a UV, skylight, Haze 1A or 1B, or a polarizer. For black and white, use a yellow filter, or, for stronger effects an orange or red filter. Any of these precautions will help to bring clarity to photographs of distant views.

USING THE FOREGROUND
When you walk down a country road, the distant view remains the same but the foreground changes constantly. One picture may have a tree in the foreground, and another a combine harvester, but both have the same view behind. The pictures above were taken only yards from one another. The foreground of the one on the left shows signs of habitation. The one on the right shows the same mountains but the hillock emphasizes the wild country.

DEPTH OF FIELD
Controlling depth of file (ie how much of the picture is recorded in sharp focus) is very important in landscape photography. If you use nearby objects in the foreground, you have to set a small aperture to keep both foreground and landscape sharp. Lenses which stop down to f22 are ideal. The alternative is to use the unsharpness that results from a shallow depth of field. Either way, use your depth of field scale on the lens or stop-down preview button to check.

FRAMING THE VIEW
To avoid too much blank sky or if you want to exclude a distracting foreground, find a suitable frame for the view. Use a tree or an arch, making sure that the frame does not attract more attention than the scene itself. By including the area where the frame and landscape meet, the shot gains depth.

THE RIGHT LIGHT
A scene that impresses you because of its sense of space and scale may often lose its impact in a two-dimensional photograph. Look at the shots above: the sunlit scene on the right is much more colourful than the picture taken when the sun was obscured, yet the two shots were taken within a few seconds of each other.
Strongly-angled light can help give the landscape more depth, picking out the texture of a ploughed field, for example, and throwing details into sharp relief. If the light is dull, confine your landscape pictures to scenes with foreground interest or return when the light is stronger.

COMPENSATING FOR THE SKY
Exposure readings are crucial. When the sun is shining, use your normal overall reading from the TTL meter. When it is not, the fact that the sky remains bright causes the TTL meter to under-expose the duller landscape.
In both the above shots a normal TTL meter was used. As a result, the picture taken when the sun was behind the clouds is under-exposed. To restore full exposure to foreground detail, aim the camera downwards and take your reading from the ground, leaving out the sky. If you are in doubt about the reading, bracket your exposures, but always err on the side of over-exposure.

Better pictures in bad weather

Don't assume that the best pictures are always taken on bright, sunny days. Landscapes and city scenes benefit from dramatic weather, rather than good weather. A change in the weather means a change in the quality of the light, and light is what creates shape and texture, colour and contrast in your pictures. Often the best weather for photography occurs in changeable conditions.

Rain brightens textures and reflects back the light so that dark, dull or flat surfaces become glossy and show detail.

Snow hides small, distracting detail and smooths the overall shape of the land.

Fog masks detail too, and increases the feeling of depth in a picture.

Wind sways trees and grass in a common direction, and improves pictures of falling rain or snow.

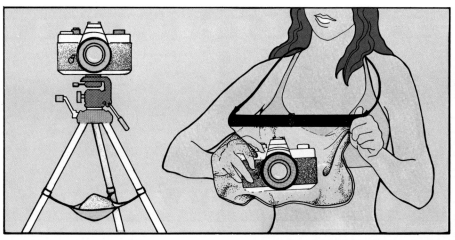

SECURING YOUR TRIPOD
A tripod with spiked feet helps to give a secure grip on wet ground or in wind. Some types have wide-splayed legs for extra stability. In wind, fill a bag with heavy stones and sling it underneath your tripod. If the wind is strong, keep the neckstrap on, even when the camera is on the tripod, in case it blows over. Use your body to shield the camera from high winds during long exposures and to cut down vibration.

WEATHERPROOFING YOUR CAMERA
There are some ready-made weatherproof cameras, but these are not SLRs. To protect an SLR against rain, snow or spray, you can buy a housing intended for underwater photography. It is bulky to handle but gives complete protection. Otherwise you can buy a weather cape which opens at the back for film changes, or use a polythene bag over the camera with the lens protected by a filter.

SNOW
Bad weather tends to keep many photographers indoors. But snow brings about such dramatic changes that the landscape becomes a subject in itself. This transformation requires different camera techniques. First, you can afford to load your camera with slower film because the snow reflects the daylight, boosting the light level. Second, you can no longer use your TTL exposures for bright sunlight, without adjusting them. Presented with large areas of white, your TTL meter will recommend exposures that would reduce white to mid-grey. For white snow give two stops extra exposure. For correct skin tones, take a reading from your hand in front of the lens.

MIST AND FOG
As with snowscapes, pictures taken in fog require more exposure than the TTL meter recommends. Open up by one or two stops to keep the mist areas white rather than grey.

REFLECTED BACKLIGHT
Look for low sunlight reflected off wet ground, and use the exposure given by your TTL meter for the overall scene. This gives the dramatic effect of objects silhouetted on bright areas.

FLAT LIGHTING

A dull, overcast day gives you a flat, low-contrast light. Colours may be colder and less brilliant, with less distinction between them. With slide film, you will get best results by giving minimum acceptable exposure. Contrast and colour will look better in a slightly darker picture, though for a softer, diffused effect give more exposure. With colour negative film in flat light, the best exposure is the one your meter recommends. A warm-up filter such as 81A will cut out the cold blue tones. A graduated filter will add a fake blue sky in place of white. Look for foreground interest.

CONTRASTY SKYLIGHT

The most difficult type of dull day is when the sky overhead is overcast but there is a window of sunlight on the horizon. The distant brightness makes everything nearby look very dark (as in the picture above) and can seriously distort TTL meter readings. If you aim away from the bright area there is no problem. However, if you want to include sunlight in your picture, you should always take your meter reading from the ground or with the camera turned away from the bright area. Be careful not to include too much sky in the final shot or flare may spoil the rest of the picture. Use a lens hood in conditions like this.

LONG EXPOSURE PROBLEMS

In winter, some days are so dark that with medium speed films, your exposures are too long to hand-hold. You will need to use a faster film – or a tripod. If you are forced to use long exposures, look hard at the scene for unwanted movement. Moving cars and people, or trees and foliage blown by the wind, can spoil your shots. Do not hesitate to use a wide aperture on distant scenes where depth of field is less of a problem. If necessary, uprate your film for shorter shutter speeds. Plan your photographs for the middle of the day and avoid the two hours after sunrise and before sunset.

FALLING RAIN AND SNOW

Using fairly slow shutter speeds you can record drops of rain and flakes of snow as they fall, as streaks across the frame. Shutter speeds of 1/30 to 1/125 will often show blur – depending on the speed at which the rain or snow is falling. For longer streaks, you will need a tripod and speeds from 1/15 to 1 second. Exposure speeds longer than 1 second will show the rain or snow as an overall grey veil and lose the effect. Speeds of 1/500 or 1/1000 will freeze the motion and look too artificial. Rain is more difficult to show than snow. In the picture above, backlighting has helped by making the individual drops sparkle. The shiny wet rail adds to the impression.

SUN AND RAIN

Strongly backlit by the sun, rain can make your pictures shine. Or with the sun behind you look for a rainbow in front. With slide films, give a ½ stop less exposure for saturated colour.

RAINBOWS

In the picture above, a 24mm wide angle lens was used. Use a long lens if only part of the rainbow is visible or if you are trying to show the colours more clearly.

Photographing in towns and cities

There is often more variety of colour and texture in a cityscape than in a country landscape.

For street-level pictures, when space may be restricted, a wide angle lens is extremely useful. On the other hand, a telephoto lens can be used to concertina the already close-packed buildings.

Every town and city has its landmarks. Including a famous building or statue helps to pinpoint the scene. But take care that your pictures do not turn into a series of impersonal, postcard-type views. Include some human interest – or find some bright, effective detail – to give your pictures some individuality.

You need no special equipment to photograph cities: only extra care with security. Don't carry your camera over your shoulder and behind you on its strap. An inconspicuous holdall attracts much less attention than expensive looking, flashy chrome and leather.

HUMAN INTEREST
In busy city streets, people are less likely to notice a photographer. With a long lens it is quite easy to catch candid groups like the one above. Shops, markets and pedestrian precincts are the best places to look.

AN ABSTRACT APPROACH
Look up at high buildings for pictures that take advantage of abstract patterns in modern architecture. Make use of reflections in plate glass windows. A telephoto zoom helps to pick out detail: this shot was taken with a zoom.

FINDING A FOREGROUND
In most towns there are large areas of blank tarmac and concrete – hardly an inspiring foreground, as you can see from the picture above. If you are using a wide angle lens, which emphasizes the foreground in any picture, an expanse of empty pavement may dominate the shot. You may be able to tilt the camera to cut out the foreground but this will also exaggerate the problem of converging verticals in the buildings in the background.

CHANGING VIEWPOINT
By changing the camera position by only a few meters and taking a lower viewpoint, the picture was dramatically improved. With a wide angle lens, a fairly small object or area will fill the empty part of the frame, and you can keep the whole picture in sharp focus. With a telephoto lens, throw objects close to the camera out of focus by using a wide aperture. This will often help by filling the empty foreground area with a blur of colour.

COMBINING THE ELEMENTS
This scene combines several elements: in the background there is a notable landmark. In the central area there is some human interest. And in the foreground, the flowers and bicycles make an interesting pattern.

10am

1pm

4pm

7pm

TIME AND LIGHT
The time of day has a more critical effect in a cityscape than in an open landscape. With high buildings lining each side of the street, the sun may reach the pavement only for an hour or two each day, and one side of the street or the other will probably be in deep shadow at all times. In the evening, when the sun catches just the tops of the buildings and only reaches the ground in large open spaces, most streets will be totally in shadow. The four pictures here were taken from exactly the same viewpoint but at different times of the day. The one above was taken at 10am with the sun over the photographer's right shoulder.

BUSY OR QUIET
Not only the light changes as the day goes by. At midday there are many more people on the streets for the photographer to contend with. In the picture above, taken at 1pm, a push-chair was parked firmly in front of the camera. Pick your time for photographing city streets with this in mind. If you want to show mainly the streets and buildings, choose a Sunday, or the day of the week when shops close early. If your intention is to show the streets busy with hurrying pedestrians, find a high vantage point (such as a window) from which to take your pictures, rather than attempting to shoot in between the jostling crowd.

SHOOTING IN THE SHADE
Sometimes it is better to wait until the street is entirely shaded than to try to expose for sunlight and shadow. At dusk, you may be able to balance shop-lights with the light in the sky.

CITIES BY NIGHT
City scenes that look drab, or are spoiled by some ugly intrusive feature by day, can come to life after dark when much of the disfiguring detail is hidden.
The picture of the fountain above, taken in daylight, is something of a failure. The colour is very neutral and the background overpowers the subject itself. The same view by night, on the right, benefits from the coloured lights around the fountain, from the street light behind, and from a scattering of neon signs. For shots like this you need a tripod: the exposure here was 8 seconds. More exposure would have shown more detail in the dark areas but allowed the lights to burn out.

CAR TRAILS
When vehicles move across a picture during a long exposure, their lights will draw trails of light across the frame even though the vehicle itself will not appear. Time your exposure so that the lights make a complete pattern, visualizing the effect.

GHOST PEOPLE
Long exposures can make people disappear completely if they move while the shutter is open. An exposure of 20 seconds will lose anyone walking across the scene. People who stop in the middle will appear as faint ghostly images.

81

Photographing inside buildings

Indoor scenes and architecture can make interesting photographs, and the techniques are not difficult. All you need are a wide angle lens, a tripod, and perhaps a flashgun. Unless you can guarantee to keep the camera level by eye, a small camera-top spirit level helps as well.

Public buildings, churches, stately homes and ancient monuments are obvious indoor subjects. But your own home is also interesting to photograph. Furniture, decorations, and the people who live there make fascinating subjects. Take a picture of your living room before and after it has been redecorated. Take shots of the view through the window as the seasons change.

Try recording a day in the life of your own household – far more interesting than a posed family portrait. Some annual photographs, such as cutting the birthday cake can become family traditions.

LEVELLING THE CAMERA
Keeping the camera level is important in most shots of interiors because of the dizzying effect of converging verticals when the camera is tilted. Some people find it easier to level the camera by eye than others. Your tripod may be fitted with its own spirit level, but if not you may find it worth investing in one which fits into the hot shoe. This helps by letting you adjust the tripod without constantly having to check the viewfinder.

CHOICE OF LENS
A 24mm wide angle is the ideal lens for room interiors. A 35mm lens (top) covers too little. With a 24mm lens (bottom) you could show three out of four walls.

CAMERA ANGLE
A camera held level at the height of your eye when you are standing includes too much of the ceiling in most rooms. If you angle it downwards, as in the shot above, the walls appear to lean outwards in an unpleasant way. The best height for the camera is halfway between the floor and the ceiling. Drop the camera to about 1 metre (3ft) if you want to include more of the floor, and use it at eye level if the ceiling is of particular interest. Shooting from the corner of a room makes it look larger. Shoot through an open door or window for extra distance, or right up against a wall with a waist level viewfinder.

VERTICALS
For this shot the camera was carefully aligned to avoid the dangers of converging verticals.
Make sure that the verticals are straight against both sides of the frame.

PEOPLE AND SCALE
A figure will give a room a sense of scale. Position the figure midway across the room. A seated figure adds to the feeling of size and space in the room being photographed.

USING DAYLIGHT

If the room is light enough, use natural daylight. Avoid including large areas of window, however, since this will influence exposure. Take your reading from part of the room that has average illumination – neither a dark corner nor an area next to the window. The chief difficulty with using daylight is when there are shafts of strong sunlight streaming through the windows. These create harsh highlights, so choose a time of day when the sun is not shining into the window, or wait until you get an overcast day.

Sometimes you can add a little more detail and atmosphere to the picture by switching on the roomlights.

USING FLASH

First check whether your flashgun covers as wide an area as your wide angle lens. If you are including a window, try to match your flash to the exposure required by the scene outside. Set the shutter speed for flash then see if you can get the same apertures that are needed for the outdoor light. If not, close the curtains. Check that there are no windows or mirrors to reflect the flash back into your lens. Position the flash above the camera, as close as possible. Watch out for ugly shadows.

Direct flash was used for the picture above: it shows more detail but lacks atmosphere. A better solution is to bounce your flash from the ceiling.

STAINED GLASS

Stand close to the window and take a meter reading from a medium-toned area of the glass. Use this for pictures of the glass, not if you want to show the whole interior.

COLOUR BALANCE

The lighting in most rooms has been arranged to make them look their best, so use it whenever you can. Photofloods are ideal for giving extra fill-in light. Or to boost the light level, you can replace the bulbs in your light fittings with Photofloods for brief periods – as long as they do not exceed the circuit's capacity. On daylight film both room lights and tungsten lamps cast yellow light, as in the picture above. The answer is to use tungsten-balanced film for these shots, or to fit a blue daylight-to-artifical light filter, which corrects the colour cast back to normal. This helps even with colour negative films.

USING A FILTER

The picture above was taken on daylight film with an 80A correction filter to remove the yellow cast – but it caused the daylight scene outside to look too blue. One answer is to frame so that you can see only the sky through the window. Another is to shoot when the light is very bright outside so that the window burns out altogether. The third alternative is that used by the movie makers – cover the whole window with sheets of yellow filter. This converts the blue daylight to the warmer colour needed for shooting on tungsten-balanced film. However, it is not essential for the light to balance.

FILTERS TO USE INDOORS

Daylight film

Window light	No filter
Flash light	No filter
Photofloods	Blue D-to-A filter
Household lamp	82C filter

Tungsten balanced film

Window light	Orange A-to-D
Flash light	Orange A-to-D
Photofloods	81A or Haze filter
Household lamp	20CC blue filter

Flashlight can be matched to tungsten light by fitting an orange-brown A-to-D filter over the gun.

Colour negatives are often automatically corrected for colour casts during printing. Therefore a filter is not essential, but will give better results than if none were used.

Colour slides always require a filter unless the film is matched to the light source.

Shooting better action pictures

Among the most fascinating photographs are those which capture movement and action. There is no such thing as instantaneous exposure: there is always some time lag. But modern SLRs with shutter speeds of 1/500, 1/1000 or even 1/2000 can freeze action very effectively. Indoors, flashguns with bursts of flash as brief as 1/12,000 do the same thing.

Field games, competitive athletics, cycling, steeplechasing, show-jumping, motor-racing and other events provide superb action subjects. Each has its moments of maximum effort – like when a sprinter passes his closest rival as they approach the tape, or when a rugby player dives for a touch down. To catch them on film is far more important than visualizing pictures and composing them with care. It pays to use plenty of film while you have the opportunity, and to select the best photographs later.

EQUIPMENT
For most action photography, your chief requirement is an SLR which gives you fast shutter speeds. A tripod is useful occasionally, but a pistol-grip is more manoeuverable.

ZOOM LENSES
At sporting events it is difficult to get close to the action and the subject is constantly on the move. On these occasions, a telephoto zoom is extremely useful.

ANTICIPATING ACTION
Successful action shots need good reflexes and accurate anticipation. If you release the shutter when you see the action reach its peak, you will get shots like the one above, which was taken too late. Between your decision to release the shutter and the moment when the shutter actually fires there is a delay of about 1/15 sec – partly due to the workings of brain and hand, and partly due to the mechanical workings of the camera. It is important to learn exactly how long it takes you and your camera to react, and to time your action shots accordingly. You can only do this by practice: until then do not try to frame too closely on a subject which is moving across the frame.

ANGLE AND SHUTTER SPEED
Movement running across the field of view requires a faster shutter speed than movement towards or away from the camera.
This means that in poor light, for example, you can still get sharp pictures of a moving subject at shutter speeds around 1/125. Even when the movement is not directly towards the camera, as in the shot above, you can rely on a slower shutter speed. This picture was taken at 1/250: it would have needed at least 1/500 if the car had been travelling at right angles to the focal plane. This point of view loses none of the excitement of action: in many sports it gives you the opportunity to catch the expressions of the sportsmen.

CATCHING THE PEAK
Every athletic action, like jumping, swimming or riding, has brief moments of hiatus – when there is least movement.
A pole vaulter at his peak of his leap is a good example: at moments like this it is easier to freeze action even if the light is too poor to allow a very fast shutter speed. Typical peak points include moments of impact in ball games, and the moment when a jumping horse – or athlete – is about to leave the ground. The top of any arc is also a hiatus point: the moment when a ball or athlete stops travelling upwards and begins to fall back to earth or, as in the picture above, the moment when a swing stops for an instant before it changes direction.

MOTOR-DRIVES AND AUTO-WINDERS

An auto-winder or a motor-drive can be an advantage, especially if you are using more than one camera. You can leave a camera with an auto-winder on a tripod with the focus preset on a convenient point, and fire the shutter with a cable release when the action occurs, without even looking through the viewfinder. Most inexpensive auto-winders take between 1½ and 2½ frames per second if you keep the shutter release down. Do not imagine, however, that this is enough to catch all the best moments: usually it is better to time each shot individually. Motor-drives are more expensive but can often shoot at 3½ to 6 frames per second. This uses a lot of film, but allows you to shoot genuine action sequences, like the one above, with less chance of missing the best moment. With sequences like this you can show the action as it progresses as well as being able to choose the best shot of the series to stand alone.

FOLLOWING FOCUS

It is fairly simple to keep a moving subject centred in the viewfinder of most SLRs: it is far more difficult to keep that subject in sharp focus. Swinging the camera round with the subject and smoothly changing focus at the same time – as it gets nearer or further away – takes a lot of skill. With a one-touch zoom lens, you have to zoom and focus at the same time, which is even harder to do.

The technique needs a lot of practice, until you are very familiar with the action of your lens. When you buy a new lens, it is a great help if the focusing ring rotates in the same direction as the lenses that you have already got accustomed to.

PRESETTING FOCUS

An easier and more reliable method of focusing on a moving subject is to preset the focus of your lens on a spot which the subject is to pass. In the shots above, the lens was focused on a stone in the road. It is still important to follow the subject in the viewfinder, but there is no need to touch the focusing ring. (It is just as easy to follow an out-of-focus image.)

When the subject reaches the exact spot where you have focused, it then comes into sharp focus and you release the shutter. If you are using a zoom lens you can preset the focal length as well, to make sure that the subject fills the frame when it reaches the chosen position for the shot.

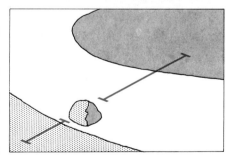

DEPTH OF FIELD

The area in sharp focus will depend on the chosen lens aperture. Work this out from the scale on the lens. Remember that the depth of field is ⅓ in front of the focus point and ⅔ beyond.

Have fun with multiple exposures

Accidental double exposures can be a disaster – a waste of two good pictures. Most SLRs have a safety lock. But you can get round this to make intentional double exposures.

The simplest form of multiple exposure is to combine two complete, separate images. Normally you can identify the whole of each image, but where dark or light areas overlap there appear extra shapes, tones and colours. Parts of each picture can disappear where the combined exposure produces pure white. But with more careful framing, you can put a small, brightly lit subject into the dark shadow area of a separate picture without affecting the rest. The skill here is in being able to imagine how the images will fit together without actually seeing the effect until the film is developed. Very dark backgrounds make multiple pictures easy to take for your first trials. Later on you can try out more complicated techniques.

SPECIAL CONTROLS
Many SLRs have multi-exposure switches. After taking the first shot, simply move the switch to the multi position. The lever wind then cocks the shutter without moving the film.

MANUAL METHODS
Tighten the film by rewinding until it resists. Hold the rewind crank firmly, press the rewind film release button and wind the lever: this cocks the shutter without moving the film.

SPECIAL EFFECT MASKS
You can buy special masks or mattes as part of a filter system or to fit certain lens hoods. Masks are used in pairs which correspond to one another: what one masks the other leaves open. Two shots are taken – one through each mask – on the same piece of film and the two images combine. In the picture above you can see the two masks used to give a centre-spot double exposure. Other masks allow you to expose the two halves of a single picture separately.
Exposure: measure exposures without the masks in place. As each shot exposes only part of the frame, you must give full exposure for each.

CENTRE-SPOT ONLY
This picture shows the effect of the surround mask. As it is very close to the lens it gives a blurry edge. At smaller apertures it becomes sharper.

THE FINAL EFFECT
The second mask has been used to blank out the centre spot while the surround has been exposed to produce this final picture.

HOW TO COMBINE IMAGES
Light parts of one picture will always dominate the dark parts of another. If the sky in one shot is superimposed on a dark building in another, the building will either disappear or will be overlaid with details of the sky. Highlights will show up in a combination, shadows will not. The scene in the picture above called for an exposure of 1/125 at f11 (on ISO 100 film). To superimpose it on to a hoarding, right, the photographer first under-exposed the sign (at 1/250 at f16) and then reshot the village at full exposure using his fingers as a keyhole mask. The central focusing ring is a help in lining up combined exposures in this way.

HIGHLIGHTS
The highlights in a multiple exposure will stay bright in the final result. These parts of the film have been fully exposed so no further changes in the image are possible.

SHADOWS
Shadow areas in a multiple exposure are the places where a new image will show up most clearly because the film receives little exposure in dark areas and is ready to respond to more.

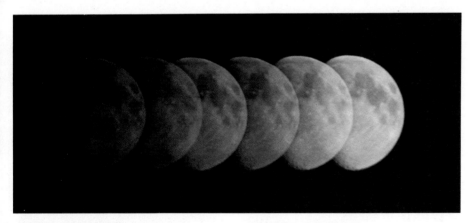

MOVING SUBJECTS
If you have a tripod, you can use multiple-exposures to record movement. With the camera still, the background scene will stay sharp while a moving subject will appear in different parts of the frame for each exposure. Time the exposures evenly so that the images are evenly spaced, and choose intervals so that there is a slight overlap. (Totally separate images will just look ghost-like.) Auto-winders can be used to make multiple exposures with cameras which allow you to keep the multiple exposure switch turned on.

CAMERA MOVEMENT
When the subject is still you can move the camera between exposures on one frame to make patterns. Give slightly less – or more – exposure to each successive shot and you will create the impression that the subject is gradually fading or accelerating. The shot above could have been produced by camera or subject movement. In fact the camera was still: the exposures were taken one minute apart to use the moon's movement. With no background detail the camera could equally well have been moved instead.

MULTIPLE EXPOSURE FACTORS

When you take more than one shot on the same piece of film, and each exposure fills the frame, each one will need less exposure.

Exposure guide
2 shots	minus 1 stop each
3 shots	minus 1 stop for first
	minus 2 stops for second
4 shots	minus 2 stops each
6 shots	minus 2 stops for four
	minus 3 stops for two
8 shots	minus 3 stops each
16 shots	minus 4 stops each

Where the exposures are uneven, you can vary the adjustments, stopping down more for the brighter subjects. But keep the overall number of stops subtracted within these limits. Where a bright subject is superimposed on an area of total shadow, or when using masks that block parts of the film, give the normal full-frame exposure for each part.

87

How to copy your prints and slides

Most photographic dealers now offer a print-to-print copying service for photographs without negatives, but it is still useful to be able to make your own copies – of prints, maps, plans, drawings or anything else that you are legally allowed to copy. Copyright normally expires 50 years after a picture was taken or, from 1957, after publication. As a basic guide, copyright law permits copying for private study or research, but not for selling.

Colour prints can be made into slides and copying can also provide a useful negative for further prints or for correcting faults in the original. In colour, poor composition – with tilted horizons, for example – can be remedied so that machine prints of the new negative come out far better. In black and white, brown/yellow stains or fading can be corrected: a blue filter will improve faded prints and using an orange filter will make any sepia stains disappear.

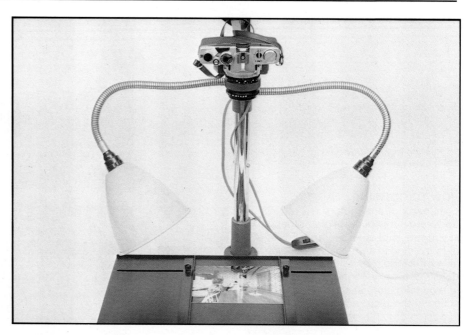

STANDS AND LEGS
Copy stands hold the camera parallel to the print being copied. The one above is inexpensive and fits any round enlarger column and baseboard. Better versions have geared mounts. Some camera makes can supply copy legs, which fit on in place of a lens hood.

LIGHTING
To light any subject for copying you need two identically matched lights or flashguns. The stand shown here uses two photoflood lamps. It is easier to get good lighting if the lights are away from the stand and fully adjustable in position and height.

Slide copying has more creative potential than print copying. It is also easier to improve a badly exposed slide than a badly exposed print by copying it. Slides contain far more information than prints and a badly under-exposed slide can often be rescued by giving it extra exposure through a copier. The equipment you need is less elaborate and less expensive than for print copying.

You will need no special lighting, though a flashgun will be useful. You can even use daylight, though this is variable and gives rather unpredictable results. There are copiers which fit bellows systems, ones which fit directly onto a standard lens and others which have their own lenses and fit onto an SLR body. Zoom or bellows copiers provide greater flexibility, enabling the main subject to be more tightly cropped or sections enlarged.

SEPARATE COPIERS
Separate copiers need no bellows, but they cost more.
Fixed focus types make slides which are nominally the same size as the original, but in fact they magnify slightly. This is because slide mounts crop ·5mm (1/500in) off the edges of a slide, and this intruding mount edge must not be allowed to appear as a frame round the copy.
Copiers like the one above have a zoom, enabling you to close in from life size (1:1) to 1:2, so that only ¼ of the original slide now fills the frame, giving a selective crop.

BELLOWS COPIERS
Most extension bellows can be used to copy slides. You attach the bellows to an SLR camera body, fit the lens to the front and then connect this by more bellows to the slide holder. Use either daylight or tungsten.

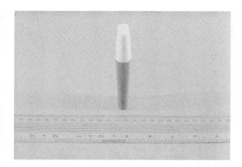

SETTING UP
To get the camera parallel to a flat subject without a copy stand, place a pocket mirror on top of the subject. Looking through the viewfinder, adjust the camera so that the reflection of the lens is exactly central in the viewfinder. Use the central focusing aid to help you. Then, to light the subject, have the two lights equally spaced on either side of the narrower edges of the subject. If there are reflections or diffused glare, position the lights lower. Use the pencil test (shown above) to check the shadows to make sure that the lights are symmetrical. If the two shadows cast by the pen or pencil seem to be the same density at equal distances from the centre, then the lighting must be fairly even.

MAKING A TEST
To test your copying set-up, use a flat subject with good colours and a matt finish – something that you will be able to compare with the finished copy. You can buy a commercially made colour checker, or make one yourself (like the one above) to find out what adjustments you will need to make for your regular film.

Do not expect perfect reproduction of all colours the first time. Correct colour casts by using colour printing filters or colour compensating filters. Make notes of all your test shots, altering the exposure by half a stop at a time. Once you have found the best copying exposure and filters, record the distances of your copy lights so you can repeat successful results.

ELIMINATING STAINS
Old black and white prints may have brown stains. They can be removed, as shown above, by copying the print through an orange or red filter on to fine grain film. A blue filter restores contrast to faded, yellowish prints, but will show up stains badly.

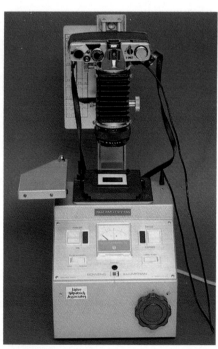

COLOUR AND CONTRAST
For exact copies, it is best to use special copy film. But this only comes in bulk lengths and unless you are making a large number of copies it is not worth loading into cassettes. Kodachrome 25 is a good alternative. Copying slides on to normal slide film increases contrast, loses some of the sharpness and may slightly change the colour. You can adjust the colour (or correct a colour cast in the original slide) by using filters. You can also adjust the final effect by changing exposure over a wide range. The two slides above show a one-stop change in exposure during the copying.

LIGHTING AND EXPOSURE
Daylight slide film gives the best results with electronic flash. Position your flash about 40cm (20in) from the opal diffuser behind the slide in the copier and make a series of test exposures: with bellows copiers try different f stops and with separate copiers try different distances. Record the details of each and compare the results with the originals. You can also use a photoflood bulb and tungsten balanced film such as Ektachrome 50. Meter the amount of light with your TTL meter in the normal way to find out the correct exposure, but always bracket exposures for important copies.

BENCH COPIERS
These use either flash or tungsten light. This one has its own bellows and copying stand.

Creative afterwork on slides and prints

There are many ways of using parts of photographs to create new pictures, or of simply changing a print by colouring it. Two or more photographs can be combined; details can be removed; new elements can be added. All these changes mean a loss of the pure photographic representation, though the results can be copied or reprinted to look quite natural.

Combined images are made in two basic ways. Superimposition is a photographic technique and requires two pictures which, when double exposed on to one frame, form a new image. Montage involves cutting and assembling parts of pictures in a sort of jigsaw image.

Coloured images can involve changing all or part of the image, or even concealing parts of it. You can also add tints to a black and white print. If making monochrome prints specially for tinting, make them light in tone and with a softer contrast than usual.

CUTTING AND MONTAGE
For print montage you will need a pair of very sharp scissors (like the ones in the picture) or a craft knife and cutting mat. Spray Mount adhesive is easy to use, and allows you to peel off and reposition the elements freely.

COLOURING PRINTS
Special photographic tints are made in both gouache (opaque) and watercolour (transparent) forms. Photo oil colours are semi-transparent. Felt-tip markers and overhead projector colouring pens are also useful.

CUT AND PASTE MONTAGE
You do not need your own darkroom for cut and paste montage. Simply look out your spare prints and select suitable ones which promise to make an interesting combination. Then make traces of them with tracing paper to check whether your ideas will work and fit together. Cut the picture elements out using very sharp scissors or a craft knife and paste the backs lightly with Cow Gum or Spray Mount.
Mount the elements of your picture onto board, slightly overlapping them. This was done in the picture on the right, and the join is hard to see. For even better results, slice through both pictures at once with a craft knife, before sticking them so that they make a perfect join when stuck down.

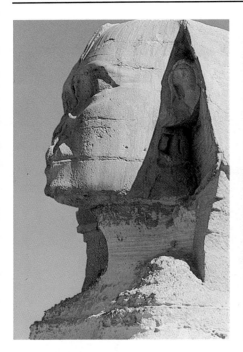  

SLIDE SANDWICHES
The two pictures above have been chosen to work as a superimposed picture. If you want to use a slide with mainly light detail and superimpose a darker element, you need not do it in the camera. Simply buy a glass slide mount

and bind both frames of film together as a sandwich. Typical examples of this could include putting an aeroplane into an empty sky, or a sunset behind a silhouetted skyline with a plain sky. A slightly sharper result is obtained with the emulsion sides together.

CHOICE OF PICTURES
Avoid complicated slides or prints when making copy superimpositions. At least one of them should be very simple, like the middle picture in this case. This means that you need only concentrate on positioning one part of the slide.

PHOTO COLOURING
The green on the left is photo dye. The sky is white gouache mixed with blue dye, and the boys are painted over with several opaque gouaches.

RETOUCHING AND DYEING
The tree on the right was done with felt-tip. A white cow was removed with grey gouache. The burning bush was made with opaque white and clear tint.

PHOTO COLOURING IDEAS

Effect	What to use
Strong colour	Undiluted photo tints; felt-tip pens; food dyes; indian ink
Conceal detail	Photo gouache; acrylic paint; oils; Snopake and dyes
Improve colour	Photo retouching dyes
Remove blemishes	White gouache overpainted with tints
Black and white	Soft pencil (2B)
Overall colour	Immerse in dilute photo tint or food dye; cover with plastic film
Coloured border; pick out detail	Felt-tip pens permanent OHP pens

Storing your slides and negatives

Unlike prints, slides are irreplaceable if damaged. Poor processing will spoil a slide for ever, so use the best company you can find or afford. Mounted slides can be stored in three different ways.

In boxes: you can leave slides in the boxes they are returned in, removing them every time you want to project them. Always label the tops of the boxes.

In magazines: the slides can be put in order into magazines ready for projection, or into boxes with slots from which they are transferred into the magazines.

In plastic sheets: file your slides in clear plastic sheets in a ring binder or suspension file. This way you can hold up a sheet of 20 or more to the light (or lay the sheet on a light box) and see all the slides at the same time. Always make sure you store your slides in a cool, dry place to prevent fading.

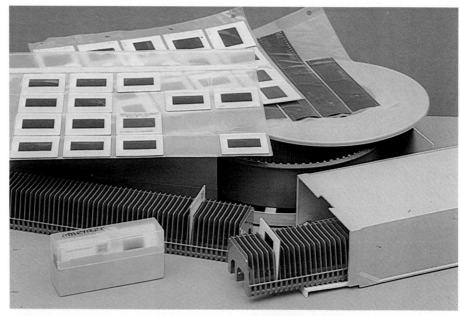

BOXES
The film-maker's own boxes take up the least space. Transfer trays, like the circular one shown here take up most. Projector magazines are a good compromise.

FILING SHEETS
Plastic filing sheets vary in size and cost. Choose ones that fit either ring binders or suspension files and stick to these. You can also buy special carrying cases for suspension sheets.

Negatives are normally kept in their original strips. For convenience, 20-exposure films are usually cut into strips of five and 24-exposure and 36-exposure films into strips of six. To make it easier to find a negative, give each film its own number and keep a complete record of where the negatives are by subject and by date. Never split up complete films. There are two main methods of filing your negatives.

In bags: each part of the film is kept in its individual bag and the strips are kept together in a card folder.

In a filing sheet: you can buy negative filing sheets in various sizes which fit into a ring binder.

With the first method it is easier to lose one strip, but the ring binder sheets need more careful handling and cost more. Whichever method you choose, make sure that the negative holders are carefully labelled and are stored away from heat.

CONTACT SHEETS
Contact sheets can be made from all kinds of negatives and also from unmounted slides. They cost about the same as a package of enprints from a film. (In the picture above the contact sheet is from a medium format roll-film camera.) If you attach a sticky edge strip to the sheet and punch holes in it, you can keep the contact sheet next to the negatives in a ring binder. In your darkroom, you can make contact sheets from negatives kept in plastic filing sheets – like the top one in the picture – without removing the negatives. Paper negative filing sheets are cheaper, but do not allow you to do this. You have to remove the negatives to make your contact sheet.

PRINT AND NEGATIVE FILES
Because contact sheets are expensive – unless you can make them yourself – you may prefer to use a system which keeps the processed prints and negatives together. The picture above shows a print and negative file. Each file will hold eight sets of prints separately, and in the drawer underneath you can keep folders with individual negative strips inside. As long as you still have the print you will be able to find the negative. Write reference numbers on each print, and the same on the negative filing wallets. The largest print size the file will take is 5 × 4in. You can also buy albums which have a pocket at the back to hold the negatives in, but these will hold fewer pictures.

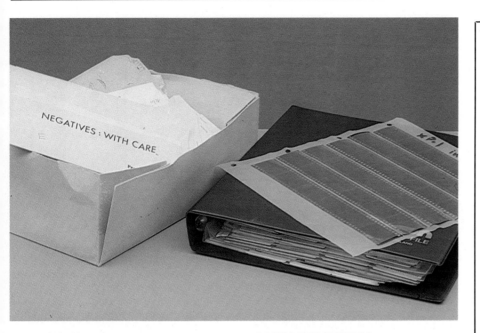

THE WRONG APPROACH
The shoebox system, above left, is no help in finding your negatives. If you keep your negatives in the individual strip bags, make a proper filing drawer or box for them.

A COMPLETE SYSTEM
The ring binder, above right, is larger than a normal office binder. It holds all your pictures, negatives in sheets and all the slides, either mounted or unmounted.

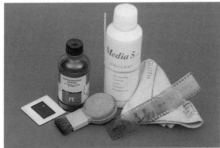

DATA BACK REFERENCING
The more slides you collect, the more difficult it is to remember when they were taken. Kodak cardboard mounts are a help as they have a date which tells you when the slide was processed – but not when it was taken. A data back, available for many makes of camera, prints a small day-month-year code (or other form of annotation) at the very edge of each shot, as shown above. On a normal enprint, the figures are about 3mm (⅛in) high. These figures are permanent and can never be erased when the slide is remounted. Some databacks print the figures rather too prominently, however, and spoil the picture. It is often better simply to keep a record of the shots you take and write the dates on later.

CLEANING SLIDES
Too much handling makes your slides dirty. You can protect slides by putting them in glass or plastic mounts, but always clean them first. Blow the dust off with a blower brush (lower centre) or aerosol jet (top centre). Wipe any fingermarks, like the one on the right, with a soft cotton pile cloth – which must be washed frequently. Use film-cleaner solutions for really stubborn greasy marks, but always remove the slide from its mount – particularly if it is a hollow plastic mount – before you do so. You can mask scratches with a lacquer like Repolisan (top left). These cleaning methods can also be used for negatives, but go gently. Usually a blower brush should be enough.

Learn to use depth of field

Look through your SLR viewfinder and study the way the image changes as you focus on objects nearer to and further away from the camera. See how much of the image behind and in front of the object you are focusing on is also in sharp focus. Then – with your finger on the depth of field preview button – change your aperture setting and look again.

Depth of field is a term which describes how much of the picture is in focus. If the scene is only sharp in one small part and the rest is blurred, the effect is called a shallow or a limited depth of field. If everything is sharp from, say, one metre (3ft) to infinity, the shot has a considerable depth of field.

The chief control you have over the depth of field of a shot is the aperture of the lens – the f stop. The wider the aperture, the shallower the depth of field as you can see in your viewfinder.

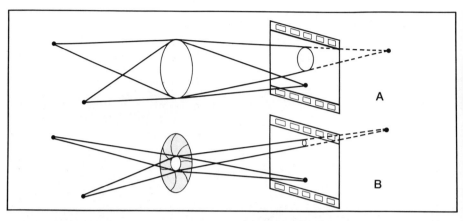

FOCUS AND BLUR
The camera lens focuses light rays by turning them into a cone which converges at a point on the film. When each point on the subject produces a point on the film the picture is totally sharp. However, subjects at different distances produce cones that converge on different planes. Light rays from a close subject take longer to come to a point. When you focus on a close object you actually move the lens away from the film: if you don't, the cone of light rays meets the film too early and forms a circle (see A).

STOPPING DOWN
The size of this circle of confusion determines how blurred the image will be. The narrower the cone of light rays when it meets the film the less noticeable the blur. Since smaller apertures admit a narrower cone of light into the camera in the first place (diagram B), they help to give a sharper image. The size of the aperture varies from lens to lens: compare a telephoto with a wide angle and you will see that its aperture is wider than the wide angle when they are set on the same f stop. Therefore, it has less depth of field.

CHECKING DEPTH OF FIELD
Depth of field is not a vague concept. It is always the same for a particular lens, focusing distance and aperture. You can check depth of field by eye. Most SLRs keep the lens at its widest aperture for focusing and framing, only closing down to taking aperture when the shutter is released. If you use the depth of field preview button or stop the lens down manually you can see how much of the shot will be in focus. Another way to check is to use the depth of field scale on the lens (see above). Fixed focal lenses have markings either side of the focus index which correspond to the f stops. Everything between the distances on the focus scale that line up with your chosen f stop is in focus.

NORMAL SUBJECTS
Unless you are using very slow film, a long telephoto, a very fast shutter speed or are focused very close, the aperture indicated by your TTL meter will give enough depth of field.

CLOSE-UPS
The closer the focusing distance, the smaller the depth of field. If you use close-up accessories to take a photograph, the depth of field scale will no longer apply.

USING WIDE APERTURES

Wide apertures give you the least depth of field. If a 50mm lens has an aperture setting as wide as f1·2 or f1·4, you can focus on a person's eyes and their nose will be out of focus. The advantage of this shallow depth of field is that you can pick out the most important part of your picture with sharp focus and leave the rest a blur – a technique known as differential focusing. But always remember that one third of the area depth in focus will be in front of the actual point of focus, and two thirds will be behind. You can check this by looking at the distance markings on your lens, closer distances will be more widely spaced.

USING MEDIUM APERTURES

The f stops in the middle of the scale on most 50mm lenses are f4, f5·6 and f8. They are often used for flash pictures, on dull days, and when action shots require relatively fast shutter speeds. They give a depth of field suitable for most subjects, though anything very close to the camera will still appear very blurred. Also, when the lens is focused on a close object, the background will not be sharp. Compared to pictures taken at wider apertures, however, the change from sharp to blurred areas is more gradual than those at medium apertures. The effect is quite natural and comfortable to the eye and benefits landscapes particularly.

SMALL APERTURES

With the lens closed to its smallest apertures – f11, f16 or perhaps f22 – everything will be sharp in most shots. Only something very close to the lens may be out of focus. These settings are most often used on bright, sunny days, or with flash for close-up work, or when using slow shutter speeds with the camera on a tripod. With every detail in sharp focus, pictures taken at these apertures are less attractive than those taken at medium apertures. There is no difference in focus between the main subject and the rest of the picture and irrelevant details can distract the eye by appearing too crisp. This calls for more care in composition.

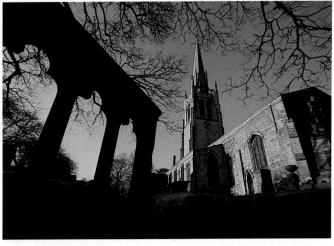

TELEPHOTO LENSES

Like close-ups, telephoto shots have a limited depth of field and require extra care in focusing. Often this differential focus is useful for picking the subject out from its background. Because most of the subject is normally distant from a telephoto lens, the problem of nearby intrusions is not serious. If something is too close to be in focus even at a small f stop, it may be better to let it blur completely at a wider aperture. Differential focus is ideal for softening the background in portraits, whether the subject is against a plain wall, paper roll or even wallpaper. Small marks or uneven texture and lighting are hidden by the blurring.

WIDE ANGLE LENSES

Wide angle lenses have so much depth of field that with small apertures you can focus on parts of the picture only centimetres away and still keep the distance sharp. The foreground is important in wide angle pictures, which look empty without nearby detail.

Use the extra depth of field with small apertures like f16 to include interesting details. A small window can be used to frame a wide angle shot whereas you would need a big archway with a standard lens. To make use of differential focusing with wide angle lenses shorter than 28mm, use a wide aperture and a close subject.

Do-it-yourself effects

You do not need expensive accessories to try out special effects in your pictures. You can produce many creative effects with domestic items or cheap substitutes for optical accessories. Creative shots rarely need to be technically perfect, so the optical quality is not paramount. The through-the-lens viewing system of the SLR means that you can easily assess the results while you manipulate whatever material you put in front of the lens.

Basic materials you can use include petroleum jelly, cellophane, coloured plastic or acetate sheets, flexible mirror plastic, small mirrors, old spectacle lenses, magnifying glasses, coloured felt-tip pens, patterned glass sheets or anything else which colours, reflects or bends light. The three main types of DIY effect shown here will all replace expensive special effect filters or lenses and each is simple to organize.

BUYING MATERIALS
The items used here, include a security wide angle door viewer, coloured filter gels and some special felt-tip pens for writing on overhead projector transparencies.

FINDING MATERIALS
You should be able to find discarded nylon tights or stockings, cellophane wrapping, petroleum jelly and adhesive tape. To protect your lens you will also need a UV or a skylight filter.

COLOUR EFFECTS
You can make your own colour effects too. There are several sorts of transparent coloured material. Plastic sheets do not give very high optical quality, but this may not matter. Gels which cover theatre spotlights are now normally made of plastic and when new are clear and unscratched. Coloured acetates are also suitable, and better quality acetates in large sheets are made for use in TV and films (sold by companies like Rosco and Lee Filters). The best optical quality comes from proper gelatin filters. Above we show a selection of coloured acetate sheets and a UV filter coloured in with felt-tip pens.

USING FELT-TIP PENS
Some of the subtlest home-made effects come from colouring a filter with felt-tip pens. Ordinary felt-tip pens will not write on glass, though some will write on plastic. Makes of spirit-based ones that will write on glass include Staeble and Staedtler. Keep an old UV filter and buy a selection of pens in primary colours to make your own graduated or multi-colour effects in any pattern you choose.
Afterwards the filter can be cleaned with film cleaner or with lighter fuel. This method can be used to colour the facets of a multi-image prism, creating overlapping colour images as in the picture shown above.

USING GELS
You can imitate split-colour or graduated filters by using sheets of acetate cut up and taped over the lens. At wide apertures, the line where the coloured sheet ends (or two coloured sheets meet) will be very indistinct, so by covering half the lens you can get the effect of a graduated filter, as above. By joining two or more coloured strips together you can make filters with separate colour sections. With a wide angle lens the sections are quite distinct, but with a telephoto lens they give the effect of variegated colour cast. You can also make a centre spot colour filter by cutting a hole in a coloured sheet of acetate.

SOFT FOCUS

Soft focus filters available on the market are very reliable – but every picture shows the same effect. A home made soft focus, however, is unique.

Overall diffusion: is produced by stretching mesh or net material like tights or stockings over the lens. Fine weaves can give strong softening effects: muslin or curtain net are clearer. Sometimes they also produce small starbursts from light sources.

Centre spot soft focus: can be achieved either by smearing petroleum jelly round the edge of a filter or by surrounding the lens with a cone of crumpled cellophane. Both can be shaped to fit around the subject.

USING MATERIAL

Stocking material should be stretched evenly over the lens on a wire frame or taped in front of the lens hood to give an effect like this. The tauter you have the material, the clearer the image.

USING CELLOPHANE

Loosely crumple some clear cellophane around the inside of the lens hood so that it intrudes into the picture area. Light is both transmitted and reflected and the effect varies enormously.

A HOME MADE FISH-EYE

This do-it-yourself project is hard to resist if you compare the price – less than a 20-exposure roll of colour film – with the cost of a manufactured fish-eye lens. It is particularly worthwhile since a fish-eye lens is only rarely used. The optical quality is by no means first class, but it is fun to use. The only materials you need are an old plastic lens cap and a wide angle door viewer, sold by home security companies. This is a small lens intended to be screwed through a solid front door to give a panoramic view of anyone calling. The quality of the images you get varies with the make of door viewer that you buy, so choose the item with care.

ADAPTING THE LENS CAP

Cut a hole in the centre of the cap (making sure that it is the true centre) and push in the door viewer. Make sure that the end does not touch the front element of the lens.

EXPOSURE

Stops smaller than f5·6 may make the circle of the fish-eye image smaller. You will need to experiment but, as a guide, use ½ to ¼ of the exposure given by the TTL.

How to use unusual views

The camera can go where the human eye cannot and shots from unusual angles make the viewer stop and look. It can be inserted through a narrow gap, aimed around corners, set up in a hole in the ground or lifted up on a skypole. The snag is that unless you can see through the viewfinder, your aim and composition must be haphazard. Some photographers go to enormous lengths to overcome this – even to the extent of attaching a video camera (with a remote screen) next to the SLR.

But you don't have to go this far to benefit from unusual viewpoints. If your SLR has a waistlevel viewfinder there is no problem. This will give you a good view with your camera on the ground or held upside down above your head. If you have no waist-level viewing facility, you can fit a simple optical viewfinder extension, which rotates the image through a right angle.

RIGHT ANGLE FINDERS
A rotating right angle viewfinder shows the full area sharply enough for normal focusing. With cheaper types the image will be back-to-front, as in a mirror. More expensive versions have a prism to give a right-way-round image.

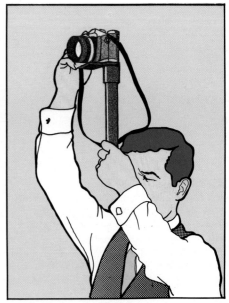

PERISCOPE FINDERS
The novel periscope finder shown here does two jobs. It screws into the tripod bush to support the SLR firmly above your head (supporting it on the eyepiece alone would damage it), and gives a view as if seen through a right angle finder.

OVERHEAD VIEWS
In crowds and at concerts you may find yourself behind a solid row of people, barely able to see through and unable to take a clear picture without intruding heads. Press photographers sometimes fit a wide angle lens and just hold the SLR at arm's length above their heads, aiming by guesswork. If you have a waist-level viewfinder hold the camera upside down and use the finder to compose the shot – but first, check that your particular SLR will work properly upside down. A periscope finder is a great asset if you take a lot of pictures this way. You can also try jumping up and shooting at 1/1000 to prevent your own movement from blurring the picture.

FRAMING WITH A FINDER
The image you see is reversed. This means that you have to tilt the camera in the same direction as the tilted horizon on the screen to get it level. Pictures with a vertical format are difficult to frame correctly.

AIMING BLIND
You may find you can shoot more quickly by guessing your aim. This is particularly useful if you are shooting negatives which can be cropped later to correct any tilts. Take a series of shots like this from different angles.

WHY CHANGE THE VIEW?
The shot above is of a fireman who has just dropped down the polished pole in a fire station – a swift and dynamic movement. It is not in fact an action shot: the light was strong enough for an eposure of only ¼ at f2·8 with a 35mm lens. But nevertheless, the shot could have implied more action than this static close-up. A change of viewpoint can make even a posed shot seem far livelier, as the following pictures show. These were taken with the same lens and existing light. No dramatic lighting or wide angle effects were used. The only changes were in the position of the camera and the subject.

FROM BELOW
In the shaft where the fire crew slide down to their machines, the light comes from above. Shooting from below means that reflected light is picked up from the pole and the walls of the shaft and the fireman is left in silhouette. In this case the low viewpoint was in fact at eye level and no special finders were required. The shot was taken at ⅛ at f4, the fluorescent lighting giving the picture a greenish cast. Despite this the picture is visually interesting. The figure makes an unexpected shape because of the change of perspective and the camera tilt makes the parallels seem to rush away.

FROM ABOVE
Looking down on the fireman is as effective as the low viewpoint, though more familiar. It seems more natural for the head and hands of the figure to dwarf the feet than the other way round. The available light is not so interesting but it has better colour quality. Normally, most light comes from above so, in general, low view shots are often either badly lit or in silhouette whereas high view shots tend to be fully detailed. Again, converging verticals – the result of pointing the camera downwards this time – give a strong impression of movement though the fireman was, in fact, stationary for the shot.

SHOOTING AT GROUND LEVEL
Ground level views are fascinating – more unusual than high viewpoints since we rarely put our faces that close to the ground. An SLR can go even lower than the eye: use a waistlevel finder or right angle attachment and kneel or squat down to compose the picture. Use a beanbag to settle the camera firmly on the ground. Mini tripods or groundspikes will also support a camera from 3cm (1¼in) above the ground. A ball and socket head fitted with a metal spike holds a camera in any position and is ideal for flower shots. You can use a cable release to fire the shutter.

CLOSE-UPS
Most ground shots either look sharply upwards or are close-ups. As above, even in good light, shots taken this close will have a limited depth of field, but this is acceptable with the odd angle.

PEOPLE
Low level views of adults look dramatic – but they are seldom flattering. Babies and children viewed from their own height look more natural and in proportion.

99

Shooting pictures in sequence

Picture sequences are fascinating because, like movie film in slow motion, they show stages of an action which happen too quickly for us to see properly. Sequences can tell a story, or even a joke. Or they can break down a process or action into a set of interval-timed shots, for which you will need some extra equipment or technique. For stories all you need is imagination.

Here we look at the technical side of timed sequences – how to time the interval between shots so that the sequence is not only interesting but also reveals something about the subject. Slow sequences can be timed with a wristwatch. Fast sequences need an autowind or motordrive: even if you can wind on very quickly by hand, you run the risk of altering the framing. Motordrive units are also helpful where the timing is crucial because they are able to release the shutter at an even pace.

WINDERS
If the action you are shooting is very fast, you may need a motordrive which takes between 3·5 and 5 frames a second, or an autowinder that takes between 1·5 and 2·5 frames a second may be sufficient.

TIMERS
If you are not able to wait with the camera and release the shutter manually at timed intervals, an intervalometer will fire the motordrive for you. These can be bought separately.

TIME LAPSE SEQUENCES
Time lapse is a term used by film makers. It describes a process whereby individual frames of film are shot at a rate of one per second or less, and then projected at 24 frames per second. This contracts time so that slow events – like flowers opening or clouds moving – seem to happen quickly. In still photography you can imitate time lapse by taking pictures at long intervals and displaying them in order. Each picture should be taken from an identical viewpoint. Either leave the camera fixed on the tripod or buy a quick-release tripod mount. Half of this is fixed to the camera and half to the tripod so that the camera can be positioned accurately.

MANUAL TIMING
The sequence above was timed manually.
It took several seconds for the fresh coal to catch light, and the shots show the decisive moments in this process. First the heavy smoke, then the appearance of flame, then the moment when the whole fire began to burn. The camera remained fixed on a tripod, and the whole sequence showed all the changes until the coal was burned away. If a precise, scientific analysis had been required, the shots would have to have been timed at accurate intervals. Look for subjects outdoors too: changing shadows during one day or flowers that turn to face the sun.

USING AN INTERVALOMETER
Unless you have a special adaptor, you can only use an intervalometer with an electronic shutter release camera. You will also need an autowinder to wind on between frames. Inexpensive autowinders give times between one frame per second and one per minute. With a set-up like this, using flash or auto-exposure to make sure of the right exposure you can leave the camera unattended in a safe place to make the sequence. If your camera has an electronic delayed action timer, you can get a 10 sec interval by leaving it switched on and using an auto-winder, with the shutter release lock down with a cable release.

ACTION SEQUENCES

Unless the action takes place in a totally predictable place, hand-hold your camera and use an autowinder. Not all SLRs will accept one of these. Auto-exposure helps too, if the light changes during the sequence. Remember to use a fast shutter speed to freeze the action, and choose a lens with a wide enough angle to accommodate the subject if the action is unpredictable. If the action takes place in a fixed position – as with gymnastics, for example – you will be able to use a tripod. You will also be able to wind on by hand, since you will not need to use the viewfinder and winding on will not distract you.

STATIC TECHNIQUE

In the sequence above, the camera was hand-held. The commandos were staging a display of self-defence techniques on a rubber mat, but nevertheless soldiers sometimes rolled off the mat and required a slight change of camera position. The pictures were taken at two frames per second. In a professional study of the technique of self-defence, the intervals would have to have been shorter to show enough detail: the change between frames 10 and 11 here is too great. But for general interest the speed is quite sufficient. Any less difference between the shots and the viewer would get bored.

PANNING TECHNIQUE

With highly mobile subjects you need to pan during the sequence. Follow the subject through the action, and keep the shutter release pressed down at the same time, using an autowinder. Make sure that you have enough depth of field, setting a small aperture, since it is difficult to pan, shoot and focus at the same time. If you can predict the line the action will take, use the depth of field scale to work out the best focusing point beforehand. Take a general light reading and set this manually: with an auto-exposure camera, avoid auto when the background changes from dark to light or the exposure changes.

ONE-FRAME SEQUENCES

Sequences can be expensive to shoot as they use a lot of film. You can make a sequence all on one frame, however, if your camera has a multi-exposure switch like the one shown here. It will work best if there is a good deal of movement between shots: small differences overlap too much to show clearly. Choose a subject that is lighter than the background rather than darker. Above all, make sure that the camera is firmly fixed on its tripod. Random actions do not work well in a one-frame sequence. Choose a mechanical action, like the swing of the transcription arm over a record deck, as demonstrated here.

SUBJECT CONTRAST

Contrast in colour is not enough to make sure the subject stands out. If you have no suitable background, choose a well-lit subject against a background of deep shadow.

CALCULATING EXPOSURE

For two exposures, give one f stop less than normal for each. For three, give one-and-a-half. For four, give two f stops less per shot and so on. (See the table on page 87.)

101

Darkroom improver course

Once you begin improving your pictures, you will want a new direction for your hobby and there is no better place to go than into the darkroom. There, completely different challenges and pleasures await.

Continuing on the same practical theme, this section has been compiled to guide you through the basic stages of developing, printing and enlarging. There are sessions dealing with building a darkroom, film processing, making contact sheets and black and white prints. Taking you a stage or two further, there are courses on printing controls, retouching, toning and sandwich printing.

Finally, to prove you have arrived, the last session takes you through the stages of making exhibition prints. There's nothing like the impact of a big print to spur you on to greater things.

Building a darkroom

If you decide that you want to become seriously involved with processing and printing your own photographs, then it's well worth your while building a permanent or semi-permanent darkroom. You could use a spare bedroom, a disused coal store or even a dry cellar (providing it has good ventilation).

Another possibility is the garage. You can separate off the last 1·5-2m (5-6ft) at one end. This gives you an ideal shape darkroom: long and narrow. You can set up a long bench and have all your chemicals and processes arranged along it in sequence from left to right.

The darkroom here was converted from an old cowshed. Part of it was divided off with a plasterboard wall and all the remaining walls were covered with plasterboard. The existing floor was concreted to create a level surface and later covered with a vinyl covering. The fittings were added later.

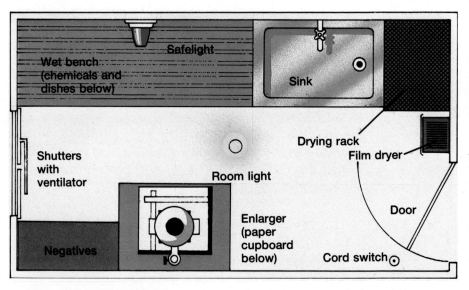

1 PLAN YOUR DARKROOM
Draw up a plan to decide how you are going to arrange everything. Most people work from left to right, or clockwise, so arrange your processes to conform to this. Also, try to keep wet and dry areas separate, as far as possible, and reduce the amount of moving you have to do by using both sides of the darkroom.

Above is a typical darkroom layout for a small room with running water. The first thing you come to is the enlarger. Moving clockwise round the room, you pass the processing bench, washing facilities and the drying rack. The dry area (enlarger, paper and negatives) is on one side of the room and the wet area (processing bench, chemicals and washing area) is on the other side.

2 A TYPICAL DARKROOM
The enlarger usually sits where the camera was positioned to take this picture. At the far end of the room a simple wooden framework holds a large darkroom sink with both hot and cold water. Because of the pale paintwork, a single orange safelight with a 15w bulb provides enough light.

There are power points above bench level and a central heating radiator under the bench to help keep dishes warm in winter. The cold pipes are lagged to stop condensation forming and dripping on to the prints or negatives. A ventilator has been attached to the outside wall to remove unpleasant fumes when mixing chemicals.

3 BLACKING OUT THE ROOM
The best black-out comes from a well-fitting door, light-tight ventilator and no windows. If your door lets in light, apply heavy, black industrial foam tape around the edges to seal out the light. But make sure you have some kind of ventilation before you do this because this type of tape also seals out the air.

4 LIGHTING AND ELECTRICS

This darkroom has seven double sockets with switches. None of them is near the sink area and all are placed so that the wires never have to trail very far. The light circuit is separate and is operated by a pull-cord switch. This avoids the risk of receiving an electric shock from touching a wall plate switch with wet hands.

5 STORING NEGATIVES

Negatives are best stored next to the enlarger area. Not only is this convenient, but they will be well away from the wet area. A steel shelf of the type shown here is ideal for storing negative files and other items such as focus finders and gloves. You must never put chemicals, wet processing equipment etc on or near it.

6 STORING PAPER

Don't store photographic paper on shelves; it can be quite heavy and may overbalance. Here the paper is being stored underneath the enlarger, near floor level but well away from the wet area. Down here, stray light from the enlarger won't strike the boxes directly, and the weight of the paper helps to stabilize the enlarger bench.

7 STORING DISHES

Store all dishes, tanks and colour processing baths at floor level under the wet bench. Stand the dishes on edge – they will collect less dust and you will be able to find the dish you want without having to hunt through a pile because you can quickly see their sizes. They will also take up less space

8 THE DRAINING RACK

Construct a draining rack under the sink as part of its support frame. You can use this rack to dry all your funnels, developing tanks, measures and other items quickly and thoroughly. On the floor beneath this rack you can store your bottles and containers of chemicals.

9 FLOOR COVERING

If your floor is wooden you must cover it to stop the floor boards from rotting. Similarly, concrete floors must be covered or treated, otherwise you will have problems with dust and it might absorb chemicals to be released later. A good solution is to lay down some vinyl floor covering.

Perfect processing

Processing your own film is easy. If you don't believe this then either you have never developed your own films before – or you've picked up some very bad habits when learning how to do it.

If you follow all these steps faithfully you will develop the good habits that make good processing a joy to do. Home processing can be quicker, cheaper, safer and better than the commercial kind – the advantages are worthwhile.

But there is always some risk when you start something new, no matter how careful you are. Therefore don't start your processing experiments with an irreplaceable film, such as one taken on holiday or at a wedding. The best thing is to take a practice film, and practise on that. If you buy a cheap, out-of-date roll of film from a photographic dealer, then it won't really matter if you make a few mistakes and spoil the roll.

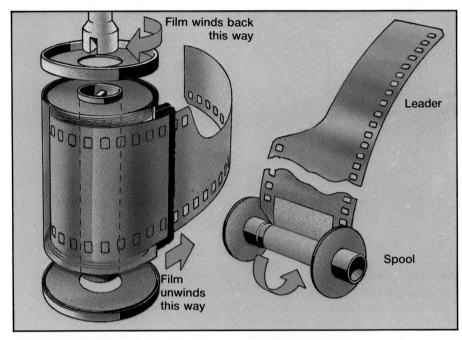

THE 35mm CASSETTE
Seen from the camera top, film is wound clockwise on to the cassette spool and unwinds anti-clockwise. The slots on the spool-top mate with the camera's rewind lever.

THE FILM
A 36-exposure cassette contains about 1·5m (4½ft) of film. One end is taped to the spool, the other end is called a leader. In a new roll the leader protrudes from the cassette ready for loading.

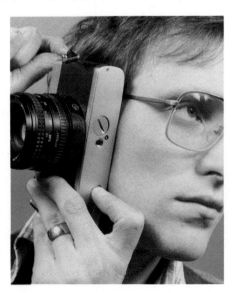

1 THE FILM ENDS
If you take a picture and wind on the film but the wind-on lever will not complete its travel, you have finished the roll of film. Check the frame counter. You can expect 25 or 26 shots from a 24-exposure roll and 37 or 38 shots from a 36-exposure roll, though you may sometimes get fewer.

2 TESTING FOR FILM
If you aren't sure that the film has finished, there's a simple way of checking. Unfold the rewind lever, but do not lift it up. Gently turn it one way until it meets resistance, then the other way. If the film is finished, you will only be able to manage half to one turn in each direction.

3 REWIND THE FILM
Hold the camera to your ear and press the rewind release button. Wind back the film slowly, listen for the first click, then stop. This way you will not wind the leader back inside the cassette and so gain easy access to the film without having to break open the cassette to reach the film.

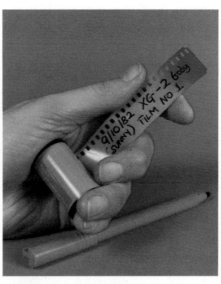

4 REMOVE THE FILM
Lift the rewind lever fully to open the camera back (or use the catch if your camera has one). Do this in shade or indoors with the camera back facing you. Remove the cassette, angling the bottom out first. Grip the cassette not the film, or you will unwind it. With the leader out, the film looks like any other roll of film, so label it clearly.

5 IDENTIFY THE FILM
Write on the leader strip so that you can identify the film later on. Do this even if you only number it instead of writing all the data shown here. Later on you will find it useful to record other details which will be helpful when you come to process it. Here, the date, camera body and weather are also recorded for reference.

6 PREVENT RELOADING
Wrap a rubber band round the used cassette to stop you re-using it accidentally. It also keeps the cassette tidy and stops the leader being pulled out. Adhesive tape can also be used for this, but the rubber band is quick and secure. Other ideas include tearing off 1cm (½in) from the leader end, or creasing it hard.

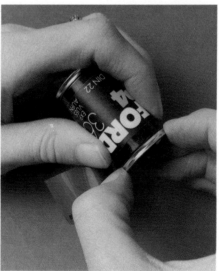

7 PROTECT AGAINST LIGHT
A cassette is not totally lightproof. Protect the cassette by storing it in the maker's film canister. (Label or put a rubber band round this as well, so you can see which film cans contain used rolls.) If you have no cans, use aluminium foil, store used film in a closed pocket of a camera holdall.

8 WINDING IN THE LEADER
If this happens, you need to break open the cassette. The red background here means it should be done in total darkness. To open an Ilford or Agfa cassette, grip it gently and squeeze the cassette together at the end next to the cap. Remove the cap, which is now loose.

A Kodak cassette is crimp-sealed at the end without the protruding knob. The best way to open one of these is to use a bottle opener on this end. You cannot reseal these Kodak cassettes, so only open them up when you are just about to develop the film, or have an old loadable cassette ready that you can transfer the film into.

107

For many people, getting a 1·5m (4½ft) roll of film into a spiral reel 9cm (3½in) in diameter means trouble. In fact it's easy once you know how but you must practice first. Do this by following the steps given here, using an outdated or unwanted film. Close your eyes when you come to the parts that have to be done in total darkness (shown here by a red background).

These reels are specially designed to hold the film spirally inside the developing tank, so that there is no chance of one part of the film touching another part. Processing chemicals can circulate freely around the film to reach every part.

A cross-section of a developing tank is shown on the right. It consists of a black plastic cylinder with a screw-on lid. The lid has a cleverly-designed light-trap so that liquids can enter, but not light. You can place either one or two reels in the tank. Here, only one is shown.

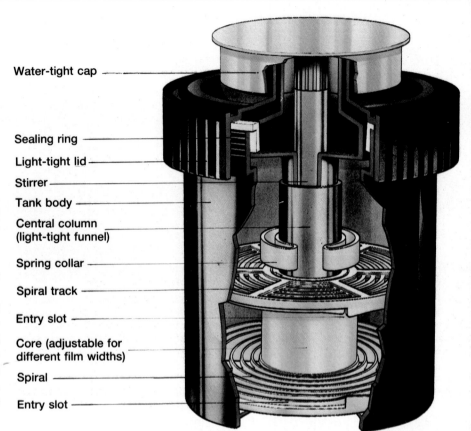

Water-tight cap

Sealing ring

Light-tight lid

Stirrer

Tank body

Central column (light-tight funnel)

Spring collar

Spiral track

Entry slot

Core (adjustable for different film widths)

Spiral

Entry slot

1 SAFE SCISSORING
The film will not go into the reel with the leader still on. It must be cut off with a pair of scissors. Get used to holding the cassette in the way shown above. Then, if you ever need to do this in the dark, you won't accidentally cut your fingers. Do not tear or crimp the cut end, otherwise you may find it jams the plastic reel.

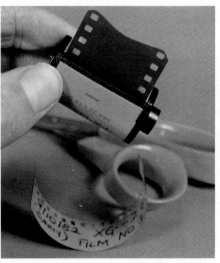

2 A STYLED TRIM
Cut the end of the film to a concave shape as shown here. This makes it very easy to load the film into the spiral reel. The rounded corners go past the outward-pointing struts of the reel without being impeded. The concave cut means that if the film end curves it does not touch other parts of the film during processing.

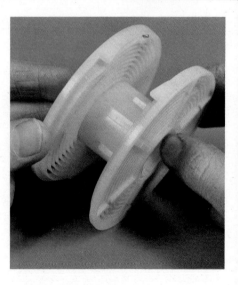

3 LINE UP THE REEL
This is the film reel. You can see the channels that the film runs along and the lugs marking the entry point. The ball bearing is part of the mechanism that grips the film's sprocket holes and pulls it into the reel. Before loading the film, line up the two entry lugs like this, then hold the reel with these on top and exactly aligned.

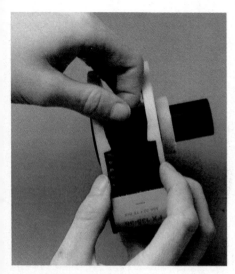

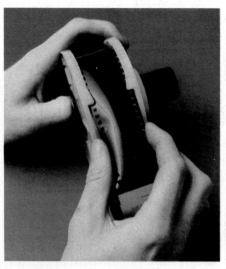

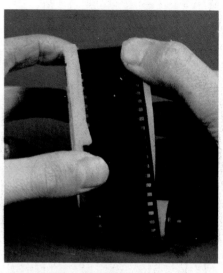

4 INSERT THE FILM
If you are loading from the cassette, you can insert the first 2-3cm (1in) of film with the lights still on. Use the grip shown here to pull the film in with your left thumb and forefinger, rather than trying to push it in. Use your right hand to hold the cassette and steady the reel. Note that there is a slight outward curve to the film – this helps it go in smoothly.

5 TURN OFF THE LIGHTS
Before you load any more film into the reel, turn the lights off (indicated by a red background here). You will now be unwinding film that has pictures on. For this trial run, close your eyes instead. Squeeze the film gently as this will probably let you enter another inch of film into the reel. Enter as much as you can. Then there is less chance of the film falling out.

6 LOAD THE FILM
Hold the reel, gripping one half in each hand. Smoothly and firmly turn the right-hand half of the reel forward, as in the picture above. Have your thumbs touching but not pressing the film. Then you will be able to feel the film being loaded. If you can't feel this happening, press down slightly on the film with your thumbs to increase the amount of pressure on it.

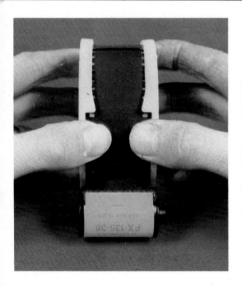

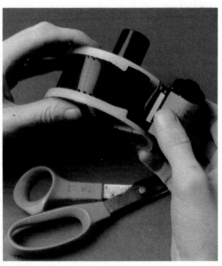

7 KEEP WINDING
When the right-hand half of the reel reaches a stop, you can do one of two things: either turn it back, or turn the left-hand half of the reel forwards, copying the first action. Whichever method you adopt, you will soon have an easy alternating action. Each forward turn grips film and feeds it in through the opposite half's entry lug.

8 DETACH THE FILM
Do this by cutting the film as close to the cassette lip as possible. But take care not to leave any adhesive tape on the film in the reel. Some films can be easily torn off just by twisting (see above), but make sure you do not pull the film out of the reel. Do not cut or tear the film until you are totally sure you have loaded all of it.

9 WIND IN THE FILM END
If you leave the film end sticking through the entry of the reel, even by a fraction of an inch, it may start to unravel during the processing. This is because the chemicals lubricate the reel and overcome its grip mechanism. Prevent this by loading the film end right past the ball bearings of both reel halves. The film will now be loose inside the reel.

Once the film is on the spiral reel, the next stage is to load this into the developing tank. This is a specially designed piece of equipment that is light-tight yet still allows the developing solutions to be poured in and out.

It contains a number of parts, all of which must be assembled correctly for the tank to work. For example, the tank contains a column called the pillar which holds the reel. If you put this in the wrong way round, the tank will not close completely and solutions will escape.

Practise the steps on a bench, and keep all the tank parts inside the developing tank while you do this. In particular, do not leave the pillar loose on the bench – it can easily roll on to the floor and get lost. Steps with a red background have to be carried out in the dark. When you're practising it's easier just to close your eyes with the lights on.

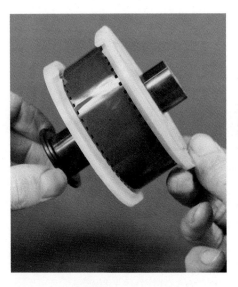

1 FIT THE PILLAR
Push the spiral reel on to the central pillar and slide it down as far as it will go. It does not matter which way round the reel goes; either way the two parts should fit firmly into each other. The pillar helps to keep out the light and, when the whole assembly is inside the developing tank, the pillar lets you stir the reel round inside the solution.

2 FIT THE RETAINING CLIP
Next fit the retaining clip over the pillar and push it down on to the reel so that the reel is held fast. When you come to develop the film you will be turning the tank over repeatedly, to wash the film with the solution, so the clip must hold the reel steady. When you aren't using the clip don't keep it on the pillar, or it may lose its spring.

3 PUT ASSEMBLY INTO THE TANK
Place the assembled reel, pillar and clip into the tank so that the reel is at the bottom. Stand the tank on a flat surface and check that the whole assembly can rotate freely inside it by giving the top of the pillar a sharp twist. Take care that you are using the right pillar if you have more than one developing tank. They can easily be mixed up.

4 ADD THE SEALING RING
This is a white, slightly soft, plastic ring that fits into the top of the tank. When you screw on the lid it gives a firm, tight seal and stops the lid from coming unscrewed during processing. It also seals the joint so that chemicals do not leak out. If the sealing ring feels loose, it can be improved by stretching it with your fingers.

5 SCREW THE LID ON
This needs a bit of care because it's easy to get the threads engaged wrongly. To do it correctly, hold the body and lid as shown here and first mate them up as closely to parallel as you can. Then screw the lid on. Do not do this too tightly, just make sure that the lid is firmly locked down. The lid is now light-tight.

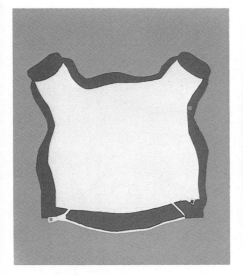

6 THE CHANGING BAG

The best place to load film into the developing tank is a darkroom. If you don't have a darkroom you can use a changing bag.
These bags are double-lined with black material, each layer having a zip so that you can get equipment inside. They also have two arm-holes to let your hands inside.

7 WHAT YOU NEED

To use a changing bag, you need the equipment shown here. Don't put anything else inside (for example, the stirring rod or water-tight cap). If the film leader is accessible (as here), trim this and start the film in the spiral reel as shown on the previous pages. (Only wind on the first inch or two. Any more and you'll be exposing film with pictures on.)

8 INTO THE BAG

The changing bag has two skins and two zips. All items must be inside both bags; only in there is it completely light-tight. It is very easy to place items in the space between the inside and the outside bags if you're not careful. After putting everything in the inner bag, zip it up. Then check the space between the two skins to make sure everything's inside.

9 SEAL THE BAG

After checking that everything is safely inside the inner bag, do up the outer zip. Once your hands are in the sealed bag, you will have to keep them inside until you've finished, and it gets warm inside! It's best to wear cotton gloves to stop your hands from becoming sticky and marking the film. Once your gloves are on, put your hands through the holes.

10 USING THE BAG

Wear a shirt or sweater when using a changing bag, since this gives a better seal round your arms. Feel all the items in the bag and clear a space before you start. Load the film on to the reel, only pulling out 25mm (1in) at a time. Work slowly and carefully. Be careful with the scissors and make sure you don't cut the bag lining.

11 UNLOAD THE BAG

Once the film is inside the tank and the tank lid is securely screwed on, remove your hands, unzip the bag and take everything out. Do not place the tank in direct sunlight, even though it's light-tight. Normal domestic lighting won't harm it, though. The next step is to prepare the chemicals you will need to process the film.

With your film loaded inside the developing tank, you are now almost ready to begin processing.

For this stage, the equipment you will need is shown in the diagram on the right.

The chemicals you need are a developer, and a fixer, though you should also use a stop-bath and a wetting agent. To show you the steps, we have used Paterson chemicals: Acutol, Acustop, Acufix and Paterson Wetting Agent. But there are others which will do just as well.

The developer, stop-bath and fixer are all supplied as liquid concentrates and need to be diluted for use. The stop-bath and the fixer can be used over and over again, so it's worth your while making up a solution of these and storing them. The developer, on the other hand, can only be used once and then discarded. So this is made up as you need it.

ESSENTIALS   OPTIONALS

For film developing, you will need: a) a measuring jug with capacity between 300ml and 600ml, b) a watch with a second hand, c) chemicals, d) a thermometer, and e) two plastic storage bottles, capacity 300-600ml.

You will find the following useful: f) a drip tray, g) a 100ml measuring cylinder, h) an accurate timer, i) rubber gloves, j) an apron, k) kitchen paper, l) an extra 300-600ml measuring jug, and m) a funnel to help in pouring.

1 THE INSTRUCTION SHEET
The developer, stop-bath and fixer all come with a set of instructions. They tell you the temperature the chemical should be at when you use it (usually 20°C), and how long you should leave it in the developing tank. This varies with different films. For examples, Ilford FP4 in Acutol needs six minutes to develop at 20°C.

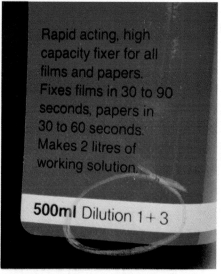

2 DILUTING THE CHEMICALS
Before you use any of these liquid concentrates, they must be diluted with water. The amount you need to dilute them by is given in the instruction sheet and on the bottle label. For the fixer the dilution ratio is 1 + 3. This means one part fixer to three parts water. The developer is diluted 1 + 10 and the stop-bath 1 + 30.

3 HOW MUCH DO YOU NEED?
For each chemical, you need enough to cover the whole film. This depends on the film size, and the size and shape of the developing tank. The base of the Paterson tank tells you how much you need for different film sizes, per roll of film. For one roll of 35mm film the figure recommended is 290ml but it is safer to use a little more.

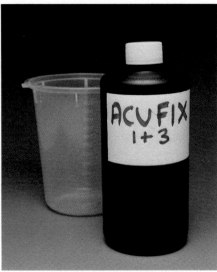

4 MAKE UP THE FIXER
Fixer keeps well, so it can be made up in advance and stored. For the fixer, 600ml is a convenient amount to make. Pour 450ml of water at about 23°C into a measuring jug, and 150ml of fixer into another, smaller jug. Then add the fixer to the water and stir well.

5 BOTTLE THE FIXER
Store the fixer by bottling it with the aid of a funnel, preferably in a special plastic bottle. Then label it. Leave a space on the label so that later on you can mark how many films you've used it for. Stick the label near the top; then it's less likely to fall off when the bottle is in water.

6 MAKE UP THE STOP-BATH
Now make up the stop-bath. This has to be diluted 1 + 30. So, for 600ml, you need just 20ml of the stop-bath concentrate and 580ml of water at 20°C. Take care when pouring the concentrate into the water – it is very acidic and will burn if it touches your skin.

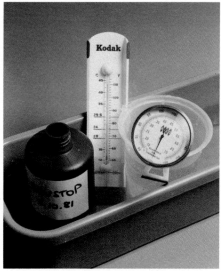

7 BOTTLE THE STOP-BATH
Bottle the diluted stop-bath in the same way you did the fixer, using a similar 600ml plastic bottle. Then label it, sticking the label at the top of the bottle. The stop-bath turns purple when it's used up. So, unlike the fixer, there's no need to mark how many films it's been used for. Thoroughly wash the funnel and the measuring jugs.

8 CONTROLLING THE TEMPERATURE
You now have both the fixer and the stop-bath ready. The developer should be mixed just before it's needed. To keep the other two chemicals at the right temperature (20°C), or to raise them up to it, put them in a basin of warm water. Stir the solutions with a thermometer until they have reached the right temperature.

9 ALLOW FOR ROOM TEMPERATURE
If you're doing this in a cold room, bring the solutions up to a degree or two warmer than 20°C. Your water-bath will now have cooled down, so add a little hot water or replace the bath with some fresh warm water. This will keep the bottles at the right temperature while you make up the developer and develop the film.

1 PREPARE THE DEVELOPER
You already have the stop-bath and the fixer standing in the water-bath, and your film is loaded into the tank. Now take 300ml of water at 21°C, and 30ml of Acutol. Mix them thoroughly. The solution will be clear and look either colourless or slightly yellow. The extra 1°C over the recommended 20°C is to allow for the temperature falling.

2 START DEVELOPING
Pour the developer straight into the tank, making sure it doesn't splash. Don't pour too quickly or air will be trapped inside the tank and it will overflow. Prevent this by holding the tank at a slight tilt to help air escape. Place the tank in a developing tray if you have one. This will insulate the tank from the cold work surface.

3 DISLODGE AIR BUBBLES
Start timing. Then slot the agitating rod into the tank top and use it to twist the reel quickly back and forth. This dislodges any air bubbles trapped at the top edge of the film. Keep twisting the rod for about 20 seconds. You can also give the tank a sharp tap on the worktop to help dislodge any air bubbles that are still trapped.

4 PUT THE TANK CAP ON
Put the white plastic sealing lid on to the tank now. Don't press it down quickly, but place it on as shown so that the air can escape. Then push it firmly down all the way – only the last few millimetres of its travel provides the water-tight seal. Without it, the developer will leak out later on.

5 INVERT THE TANK
When the timer shows one minute, turn the tank upside down. Wait until the noise of the developer draining over the film stops, and immediately turn it the right way up, then repeat. This ensures that fresh solution reaches the film. Repeat this inversion process each minute.

6 POUR OUT THE DEVELOPER
Ilford FP4 needs six minutes to develop in Acutol 1 + 10 at 20°C. So, instead of inverting the tank again at the six minute mark, remove the cap and pour the developer down the drain. Start pouring ten seconds before the six minutes is up, because the film continues to develop while you pour.

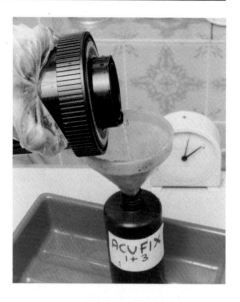

7 STOP THE DEVELOPING
At six minutes (or as close to it as you can get) start pouring in the stop-bath which you have ready. You need at least 290ml, and it's safer to use slightly more. Then agitate the solution by twisting the rod for a half to one minute. Afterwards, pour it back into its bottle. You can keep re-using the stop-bath until it turns purple.

8 POUR IN THE FIXER
Now pour in the fixer. Once again, 290ml is the minimum. Agitate the solution with the rod for 10 seconds, then agitate for another 10 seconds at the end of each minute.
With fresh fixer, the film will be fixed after 30 seconds, but it is safer to fix for three minutes. There is no need to fix for longer than five minutes.

9 RE-BOTTLE THE FIXER
Return the fixer to the bottle and mark 1 on the label. This indicates that you have used it to fix one 36-exposure roll. (For a 20-exposure roll you would mark ½.) Later on, these marks will enable you to work out when the fixer has been used up – unlike the stop-bath the fixer does not suddenly change colour. Store away both stop bath and fixer.

10 WASH THE FILM
All residues of chemicals must be washed from the film before you can dry it, otherwise the negatives will fade. Make up several changes of water at the developing temperature of 20°C in a jug and give the film 10 one-minute rinses, remembering to agitate constantly with the rod.

11 USING RUNNING WATER
If your hot and cold taps together give you running water at 20°C, you can use that for washing. It should take 20 minutes. To use colder running water, first reduce the temperature of your washes by 2°C until you reach the temperature of your running water, then use this to complete the wash.

12 EXAMINE THE FILM
Once the fixing is complete you can open the tank to examine the film: you do not need to wait until the end of the wash. Handle the film by its edges and pull out only a short amount. Normal film should look clear with images in neutral black. If it is milky after five minutes return it to fresh fixer.

1 ADD A WETTING AGENT
After washing the film, give it a final rinse in a wetting agent. Fill the tank with water, preferably distilled or ionized by a water softener. Add either five drops of a photographic wetting agent or a single drop of washing-up liquid to the final rinse water. This helps the film to dry evenly and avoids water-spotting and staining.

2 REMOVE THE REEL
Leave the film in the solution for one minute, occasionally stirring with a twist rod to make sure that the wetting agent reaches all the film. Using a wetting agent will help the water to drain off evenly.
Wearing plastic gloves, lift the reel out of the tank so that the surplus water can drain off.

3 ATTACH THE FILM
Rest the reel on the side of the tank as shown and pull out about 25mm (1in) of film. Attach a clip to the end of the film, making sure that it doesn't touch any of the images. Use a proper film clip for this; these have sharp teeth which grip firmly. You can also use a plastic clothes peg but it may slip off unless you double over the end of the film.

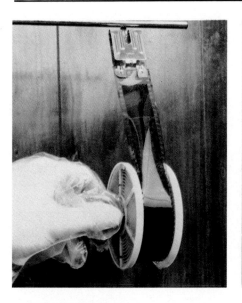

4 HANG UP TO DRY
You need a support such as a line or a rod to hang the film from. It should be at least 2m (6ft) above the floor, for 36-exposure films, and at least 8cm (3in) away from any walls. Attach the clip to your hanging point, then slowly and carefully unwind the film by turning the reel.

5 ATTACH A WEIGHT
Catch the film as it leaves the reel, otherwise it may roll up and damage the emulsion, which is still wet and soft. Then attach another clip to the end of the film to keep it taut and to stop the film curling as it dries. Put a tray or bucket underneath the weighted film to catch any drips.

6 WIPE THE FILM
The film still has surplus water on it. You can remove this by wiping the non-emulsion (shiny) side with soft kitchen paper. Do not touch the dull emulsion side. Alternatively, you can use squeegee tongs to wipe both sides at once, checking the blades for grit first and taking care not to squeeze too hard.

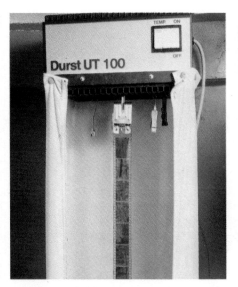

7 SPEEDY DRYING
The film must be hung up to dry in a dust-free atmosphere. One way to ensure clean, fast drying is to use a special cabinet like the one shown above. This can be closed while the film is dried by a built-in fan. An alternative is to use a hair dryer at a low setting – blow-dry the shiny side from at least 15cm (6in) away.

8 CHECK FOR DRYNESS
The bottom of the film will be the last part to dry, so check this for any spots of water. You can touch the film where there are no images, but make sure your hands are dry first. Then check for damp areas by viewing the film with light reflecting off it, as shown above. Any damp parts will look darker than the rest and drying marks will also show up.

9 COUNT THE NEGATIVES
Before you take down the film, count the number of frames. A 36-exposure roll might easily give you 37 or 38 pictures. The easiest way to store your negatives is as strips of five or six. So decide now how you will cut up your film. There might be some blanks or bad shots that you can reject to make a neat set of strips.

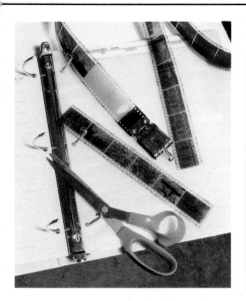

10 CUT UP THE NEGATIVES
Working on a smooth, dust-free surface, cut the film into strips of the right length. Hold the film against the light when you do this. It's a good idea to store the strips in polythene sheets in a negative file. The Unicolor file shown here takes strips of five frames, but most others take six.

11 FILE THE STRIPS
You can now insert the strips of film into the filing sheet pockets. Only handle the negatives by their edges – never touch the image area. Slide the strips carefully into the sheets, and do this over a clean worktop. Then if you drop one, it will not fall on the floor and become damaged by dirt.

12 INDEX THE FILM
As soon as you have filed the film, write on the filing sheet all the details you may want to know later on: date, subject, film type, etc. It is also a good idea to record development data, including the times and the temperatures used during processing, so you can learn from your results.

117

How to make a contact sheet

Having processed a roll of black and white film, you probably won't want prints of all the pictures. Some may be wrongly exposed or not show the subject well. But it's difficult to judge this from looking at the small 24 × 36mm negatives.

A quick, cheap way of converting your pictures to positive form without having to print them one at a time is to make a contact sheet. This is where you print all your pictures on one sheet of paper so that they come out the same size as the negatives. The images are small, but clear enough to see which are worth enlarging. But in order to make a contact sheet, first you have to make a test strip. This is to find out how long an exposure you need for the contact sheet. (Paper development is standardized, so the exposure must be accurate.)

Steps needing a safelight have a safelight symbol in the corner.

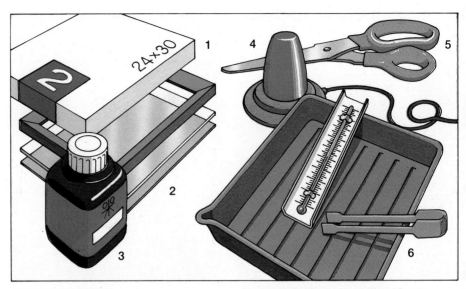

WHAT YOU NEED
1 Paper: to demonstrate the steps, we used 24 × 30cm (10 × 12in) Ilfospeed, Grade 2 glossy paper.
2 A sheet of glass: to hold the negative flat against the paper, so it should be the same size.
3 Print developer and fixer: we used Paterson Acuprint and Acufix.

4 A safelight: such as the 15watt Paterson model, so you don't have to work in the dark.
5 A pair of scissors: or safe guillotine.
6 A developing tray – slightly larger than the paper – a **thermometer** and a **pair of tongs.**
Many other brands are available apart from the ones we used.

1 BLACK OUT YOUR DARKROOM
Your darkroom, kitchen or bathroom needs to be blacked out. For windows, use a sheet of heavy card cut to shape and held in place with black canvas tape. For doors, either tape the edges or hang some black canvas. The first time, stay in the room with the lights out for at least five minutes, to see if your black-out is efficient.

2 HANG UP THE SAFELIGHT
Fix the safelight about 1m (3ft) above your work area. Don't use a stronger bulb than the manufacturer recommends. And remember, a red safelight is for black and white paper developing. It is not safe for films or colour papers. For the work area, use any clean, flat surface such as a table or a laminated board laid over a sink.

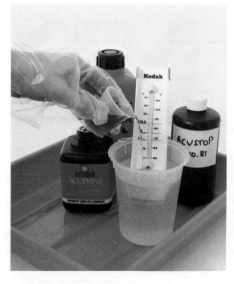

3 MIX THE CHEMICALS
Warm your existing bottle of Acustop solution to between 16°C and 22°C by standing it in a water-bath. Make up a fresh bottle of fixer (such as Acufix) at 1 + 3 dilution. Label this Print fixer – keep it separate from your film fixer and use it only for paper. Finally, take 500ml of water and add 55ml of Paterson Acuprint developer.

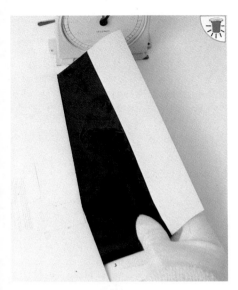

4 OPEN THE PAPER
Turn the white light OFF and the safelight ON. Unseal the Ilfospeed packet. Inside you will find a black polythene packet containing the printing paper. Remove one, using cotton gloves if your hands are sticky. Fold the polythene packet and return it to the other packet, opened end first.

5 EXAMINE THE PAPER
Look at the paper under the safelight to see which is the emulsion side. You will see that one side is glossy and the other is matt. The glossy side is the emulsion side, which is sensitive to light. Avoid creasing the paper, and avoid getting any fingerprints on the glossy emulsion side.

6 CUT INTO STRIPS
You will be using this sheet to make test strips. If you are using a 10 sheet pack of paper, cut one sheet into nine strips, each about 3cm (1in) wide. You now have one test strip for each sheet of paper in the packet. Put eight of the strips back with the paper, and keep one out.

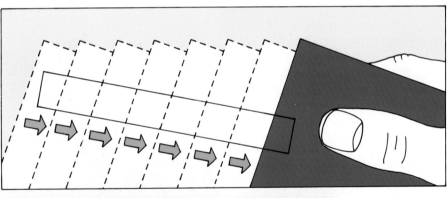

7 EXPOSING THE STRIP
Place the strip glossy side up on the bench below the safelight. Put a piece of thick card over it so that just 3cm (1in) shows. Then expose it to the light. You can remove the safelight cover to expose the strip to white light for one second (as shown above). An alternative is to switch on the room light for one second.

8 EXPOSE THE STRIP IN STAGES
Now make another six exposures of one second each, moving the card along to uncover another 3cm (1in) of the strip – exposing this for one second – each time. The easiest way to do this is to switch the light on and quickly move the card along each second. You can either count the seconds, or use a watch or clock. The digital ones are good for this.

Do not expose all of the strip, however, leave at least 3cm (1in) completely unexposed.
When you have developed this strip, you will have a grey scale extending in steps from black to pure white (the unexposed part being white) as shown above.
The next step in making a contact sheet is to process the test strip and find the exposure required.

1 POUR IN THE DEVELOPER
This is a quick way to process a test strip and contact sheet using only one tray and a small amount of chemicals. Place the exposed test strip in the developing tray glossy side up. Then pour in the diluted Acuprint developer at 20-22°C. The symbol in the corner above means that this step should be done under safelighting.

2 ROCK THE DISH
Rock the tray every five seconds to agitate the solution while developing. This is to make sure the paper is always in contact with fresh developer. After one minute, check developer temperature is still about 20°C. You can stop developing after 90 seconds. If in doubt, develop for slightly too long rather than too short a time.

3 POUR OUT THE DEVELOPER
When the time is up, pour the developer back into its measuring jug and stand it in a tray of hot water to maintain the right temperature. The test strip should show a range of tones from pure white (the unexposed part) to full black. If not, make another test, giving more exposure if it's too light or less exposure if it is too dark.

4 STOP AND FIX
Pour in the stop bath solution (which is also at 20-22°C) and rock the tray continuously for 30 seconds. Pour the stop solution back into its bottle. Pour in the fixer solution (also at 20-22°C) and again rock the tray for 30 seconds. You can now turn the light on. Fix for another 30 seconds.

5 ASSESS THE STRIP
Rinse the strip in water and examine it under white light (daylight is best). Start at the pure white step, and count the number of steps to the first step that is completely black and multiply by the exposure time. Here the sixth and seventh sections are fully black, so the exposure time is 6 × 1 second.

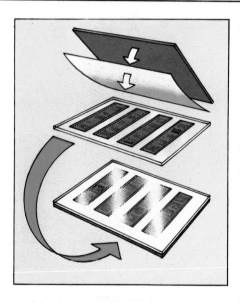

6 MAKING THE CONTACT
To make the contact sheet, the strips of negatives must be held in contact with a sheet of printing paper. The best way is to sandwich them between a sheet of glass and a piece of thick board. Build it upside down, then turn it over to make the exposure to white light, as shown above.

120

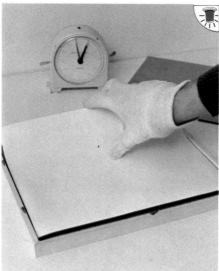

7 ARRANGE THE NEGATIVES
Place the negatives glossy side down on the glass as shown. We used a 24 × 30cm (10 × 12in) picture frame for this – this size is easy to handle and not too expensive. Wear cotton gloves, and handle negatives only by their edges. If you wish, you can write data on the front of the glass with a felt-tip pen (don't write on the negative side).

8 ADD THE PAPER
With the safelight on, take a full sheet of 24 × 30cm (10 × 12in) paper out of the packet. Place it glossy side down on top of the negatives. Be careful not to disturb the strips as you do it. Then put the hardboard or thick card over the paper. Hold it down firmly and quickly turn over the whole sandwich to reveal the negatives ready for exposure.

9 MAKE THE EXPOSURE
Place the frame on your worktop so it is the same distance from the safelight as the test strip was. Expose the frame in exactly the same way as you did the last time.
Time the exposure. This is worked out from the test strip (see step 5 above): the shortest time that produces a full black on the paper.

10 PROCESS THE SHEET
With the safelight still on, process the contact sheet using the same times, temperatures and agitation as you used for the test strip, except for fixing. As you want the contact to be permanent it must be fixed for five minutes (check the instructions for the fixer you are using). Pour away the used developer.

11 WASH THE CONTACT. . .
Wash the sheet in warm running water (20°C) for at least five minutes. If you don't have running water at this temperature, wash the sheet in 10 changes of water, 30 seconds in each, rocking the tray all the time. Do not use hot water as it can damage the print surface.

12 . . .AND DRY IT
Hold the print up by the corner to drain off water, then blot both sides with kitchen paper for faster drying. Hang the print somewhere warm, where the air can circulate freely around it. If you hang it near a radiator it will dry quickly, but too much heat will make the print curl. Dry it gently.

Making a black and white print

To make your first properly enlarged black and white prints, you must have an enlarger. This is simply a device that projects and focuses an image of a negative on to a sheet of photographic paper.

It consists of a head containing a lamp to project the image, a lens to focus it, and some means of holding a strip of negatives. This head sits on a column, at the bottom of which is a baseboard with a holder for sheets of paper. By moving the enlarger head up or down, the size of the projected image is increased or decreased to give different sizes of prints.

The figures given in this series for enlarging and exposing are based on the enlarger having a 50mm lens (the most common focal length for enlarging a 35mm picture) and a 150 watt bulb. Colour enlargers may have weaker bulbs, so if you have one of these you will need to increase the exposure times.

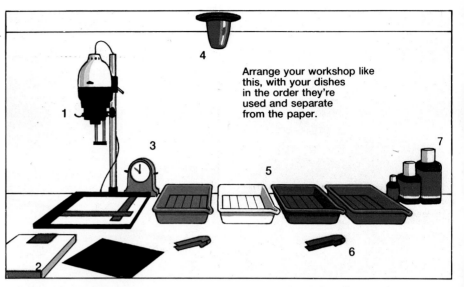

Arrange your workshop like this, with your dishes in the order they're used and separate from the paper.

WHAT YOU NEED
The essentials for enlarging are:
1 an enlarger: with a baseboard and a paper easel on it to hold the paper completely flat;
2 paper: and some opaque material for masking when exposing a test strip;
3 a timer (or an accurate watch): with a second hand;
4 a safelight.

To process the print you need:
5 three or four dishes: all 24 × 30cm (10 × 12in) – one each for developing, stopping, fixing and washing.
Arrange the dishes in the order they are used, from left to right if you are right-handed;
6 two pairs of tongs: to handle the paper;
7 chemicals.

1 SET UP THE ENLARGER
Set up your enlarger on the worktop so that its baseboard is at least 1m (3ft) from the safelight. If possible, shield the baseboard from direct safelighting. Keep the paper well away from all the chemicals and processing trays. If you are cramped for space, keep paper on a shelf above the bench.

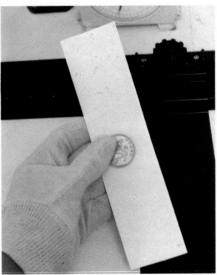

2 TEST YOUR SAFELIGHTING
Check your safelighting before you start. To do this, place a coin on a spare strip of paper, preferably a soft grade. Leave this on the baseboard for at least three minutes – five minutes would be a better test.
Then process the strip as normal, except it does not need a thorough wash.

3 IS IT GOOD ENOUGH?
Examine the processed strip. No image on it means the lighting is safe; a grey image means that it's not. To trace a fault, repeat the test with the safelight off (ie total darkness). If a grey image still appears, improve your blacking out. If not, check that your safelight is not too close.

4 FIND THE NEGATIVES
Open your file sheet and find the set of negatives you want to enlarge. Have the appropriate contact sheet filed opposite the negative sheet so you can find the negative you want by examining the contact sheet. This way, you don't have to take out a whole sheet of negatives to find the one you want, as long as they are filed in the right order.

5 EXAMINE THE CONTACTS
The images on the contact sheet are too small for you to be able to judge clearly their sharpness and composition with the naked eye.
Examine the contacts individually with a magnifier to pick out the best. A stand magnifier gives a good-quality image and, if you stand it on the sheet, the image will be automatically in focus.

6 MARK THE CONTACTS
Mark the contacts of the negatives with a Chinagraph pencil. Use any colour but red, so that it shows up under the orange-red safelight. When making a note of the negative numbers, be careful about the As. Sometimes 23 and 23A come on the same negative, but in our example, 23A and 24 come together. This is negative 24 not 23A.

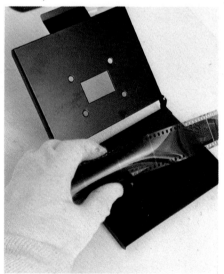

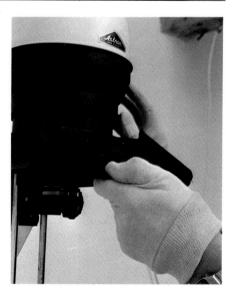

7 CLEAN THE NEGATIVE
Pick a negative you want to print and remove the strip containing it, touching only the edges. If it needs it, you can polish the shiny side of the film to remove scum marks by rubbing very gently with a soft cloth. Finally, dust both sides gently with a blower brush. Do not touch the negative with your fingers.

8 INTO THE CARRIER
Remove the negative carrier from the enlarger. Open it and insert the strip, shiny side up, with the top of the picture closest to you when the carrier is in the enlarger. Some enlargers have just a slit or a hinged head with no carrier, but the orientation of the film remains the same. Dust the carrier before use.

9 LOAD THE ENLARGER
Put the carrier in the enlarger. Once it is in, never try to pull a strip of negatives through the carrier. Some enlargers allow the tension to be slackened so that a negative strip can be moved on from frame to frame. However, it is good practice always to remove the carrier to do this.

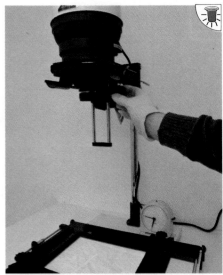

1 SET PAPER SIZE
Set the easel to take a 20 × 24cm
(8 × 10in) piece of paper. This is a
popular size, and most enlargers will
blow up a 35mm negative this big. This
can be cut from your 24 × 30cm
(10 × 12in) sheets, leaving you with strips
for testing. Set the easel to be slightly
smaller than the paper so it will hold it
flat.

2 SET ENLARGER HEIGHT
Set the enlarger so that the negative
carrier is 53cm (21in) above the
baseboard. Enlargers and lenses do vary
and you may find a centimetre or so less
gives the right size. Lock the enlarger
head (if lockable) and turn on the
enlarger lamp. Do not leave it on for
more than a minute at a time or it may
overheat.

3 VIEW AND FOCUS
Switch on the lamp and you will see an
image projected on to the baseboard.
Open up the lens to its widest aperture,
turn off the room light and switch on the
safelight (indicated here by the safelight
symbol). The image will probably be
blurred. Focus using the lens's focusing
control either by turning a knob or the
lens.

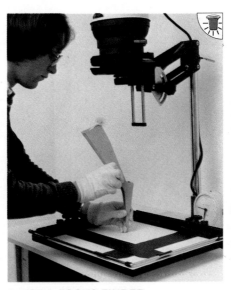

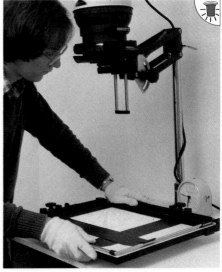

4 THE FOCUSED IMAGE
Keep moving the focusing control
beyond the point of best focus and back
until you are sure you have it exactly
focused. For the best quality prints, you
want to be precise in your focusing. As a
guide, you should be able to see the
grain clearly when the image is sharp.
Dust or fluff will also show up.

5 USE A FOCUS FINDER
Use this device if you find it difficult to
see exactly when the image is in focus.
It's not always easy if your eyesight is
poor or your enlarger has a low-power
bulb. A fine focus finder magnifies part of
the image and projects it up so that you
can view it comfortably. The highest
magnification times need good eyesight.

6 COMPOSE THE PICTURE
Move the masking frame until the picture
area contains a suitable part of the
negative. Do not try to compose the
picture by moving the negative inside its
carrier. Have the image slightly
overlapping the frame of the easel.
Check the horizon and any uprights are
parallel to the picture edge.

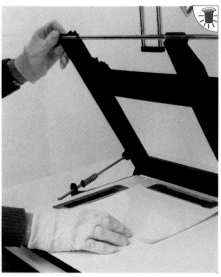

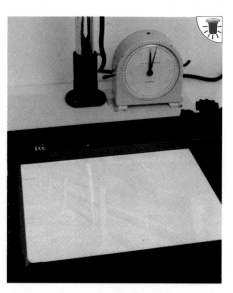

7 STOP DOWN THE LENS

Change the lens aperture from wide open (for focusing) to a smaller setting for the exposure. Set the aperture to f8, or f5·6 for small colour-type enlargers or ones with 75 watt bulbs. The smaller aperture improves sharpness and makes the exposures reasonably long, making them easier to time. Now turn off the enlarger light.

8 EXPOSE THE TEST STRIP

Place your test strip, glossy side up, over a typical averagely-exposed part of the picture. Do not choose sky or shadow areas but go for areas such as skin, grass or building detail. (We are using a full sheet here so that you can see the later steps more clearly.) The test strip is used to find out the correct exposure time.

9 EXPOSE THE WHOLE STRIP

Switch on the enlarger lamp and expose the test strip for two seconds if your aperture is f8. If your enlarger has a 75 watt bulb, give the strip a two second exposure at f5·6. For a small colour enlarger, give four seconds at f5·6, and double all the later exposure times as well. Use a watch with a second hand that's easy to see.

10 EXPOSE THREE-QUARTERS

Cover about ¼ of the test strip with card or heavy paper. Make sure the material you use is light-proof. You can use the inside of your photo packet. Give the uncovered part of the strip a further two seconds exposure. This exposure part will now have had a total of four seconds exposure.

11 EXPOSE HALF

Uncover the paper halfway and give an extra four seconds exposure.
Note that you double the length of the exposure each time. This way to get a greater range of densities on the strip, which lets you judge better what the correct exposure time should be for the print.

12 EXPOSE A QUARTER

Covering ¾ of the strip, give an eight-second exposure. You now have steps of two, four, eight and 16 seconds. One of these should be roughly correct, though you may need to pick a midway time. You can have more than four steps, but an exposure time longer than 16 seconds is rare.

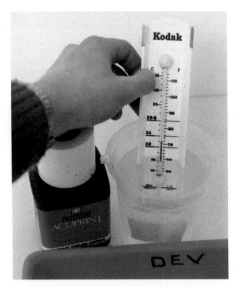

1 MAKE UP DEVELOPER
Make up fresh print developer at 22°C. You will need at least 500ml (450ml water plus 50ml concentrate) to cover the paper. This amount will process about 30 20 × 24cm (8 × 10in) prints. Then pour the solution into a clean developing tray marked DEV. If you have already exposed the test strip, do this under safelighting.

2 POUR OUT THE STOP AND FIX
Have your stop-bath and fixer in a bowl of warm water to warm them to about 20°C. (The temperature is not critical but should be over 12°C in any case.) Then pour the stop into a dish marked STOP and the fix into one marked FIX. If the dishes are coloured and marked like this, then you won't mix them up. Line them up from left to right.

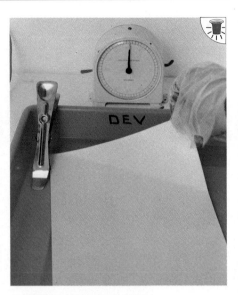

3 START DEVELOPING
With the safelight on, quickly slide the exposed test print under the developer surface, emulsion side up, making sure that it is covered as rapidly and evenly as possible. If necessary, rock the dish slightly to make the developer wash over the print as you insert it. Do not touch the developer with your fingers; either use gloves or let go of the print.

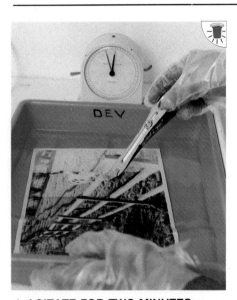

4 AGITATE FOR TWO MINUTES
Start the timer. Let the print soak for 10 seconds, then gently rock the dish by lifting the near end slightly once every few seconds, setting up a gentle washing of the solution over the print. Do this at least twice a minute, and preferably every 15 seconds, for two minutes.

5 DRAIN THE PRINT
Lift the print out of the developer. Use print tongs for this and grip the print firmly because it will be slippery. Let it drain for 10 seconds. At this stage, the print should be fully developed. Metal, plastic or bamboo tongs are all suitable, but take great care not to damage the emulsion.

6 INTO THE STOP-BATH
Slide the print carefully into the stop-bath, making sure that all the print is covered. Agitate by rocking the dish, then rinse the tongs in plain water and put them back in the developing dish. With a second pair of tongs, lift the print out of the stop-bath and drain it as before.

7 INTO THE FIXER
Put the print into the fixer, once again agitating to make sure that the entire surface is flooded with solution. This becomes very important later on, when you may want to process several prints in a row. Press the print down with the flat of the tongs. Turn the print face down and leave to fix for up to five minutes.

8 STORE IN WATER
Remove the fixed print and store it in a dish of plain water at 15-20°C. Agitate the print when you put it in, then leave it to soak. If you want you can wash the print straight away (step 9), but storing allows you to keep several prints then wash and dry them together. You will have to store them if there is no running water.

9 WASH THE PRINT
Wash the prints in running water for at least two minutes, making sure that it flows over all the emulsion surface. Check the temperature; if it is below 16°C continue washing for 10 minutes, and if at 10°C for half an hour. If you are washing more than one print, keep rearranging their order in the dish to stop them sticking together.

10 SPONGE OFF SURPLUS WATER
After the wash, speed the drying by dabbing surplus water off the emulsion with a wad of clean dry kitchen paper. Do this straight after the print has been taken from the wash, not when it has partially dried. A sharp tap or shake also dislodges water droplets, but avoid splashing nearby areas.

11 HANG UP TO DRY
Finally, hang the print up somewhere where you don't mind water droplets falling. Make sure the peg or clip that you use only touches the white border of the print. The print should be dry in about two to five minutes with heat drying, or in 30 minutes if left to dry naturally in a warm, dry room.

PROCESSING TABLE FOR RC OR PE (PLASTIC COATED) PAPERS

1	Expose the paper		
2	Develop agitate every 15 sec	2 min	22°C
3	Drain	10 sec	
4	Stop-bath	15 sec	20°C
5	Drain	10 sec	
6	Fix: agitate for 30 sec, turn sheet over	5 min	20°C
7	Drain: store in water		15-20°C
8	Wash in running water	2 min 10 min 30 min	20°C 15°C 10°C
9	Drain and sponge off water		
10	Dry		

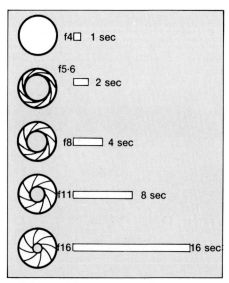

1 EXAMINE THE TEST STRIP
Wait for your test strip to dry, then assess its quality and exposure. It should have a full range of tones from clear white to pure black. Hold the print under your enlarger's light and see which step had the best exposure. Pick one which just shows detail in the whites and shadows and has good middle tones.

2 ADJUST THE EXPOSURE
Work out the correct exposure time. Here, it is between the four- and the eight-second steps, so six seconds is correct. Check that the print was sharp and if necessary refocus at full aperture. Instead of altering the time, you can adjust the aperture. Six seconds at f8 is near enough equal to four seconds at midway between f8 and f5·6.

3 APERTURE AND EXPOSURE TIME
If you want to change the aperture, (such as stopping down to increase sharpness), there is a relationship between aperture and exposure time. Increase or decrease the aperture by one stop and you must halve or double the exposure time, respectively, to get a correct exposure. For ½ stops, increase or decrease the exposure by half.

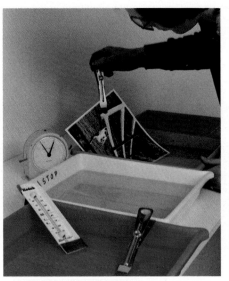

4 EXPOSE THE PRINT
Insert a full sheet of 20 × 24cm (8 × 10in) paper into the easel, close it and make the exposure that you have decided upon. We chose six seconds at f8. Use a blank card under the lens to expose the paper, this avoids vibrating the enlarger. You can also make the exposure with a switch in the enlarger circuit.

5 PROCESS THE PRINT
Follow the procedure used to develop, stop and fix the test strip. Check the temperature of the developer is above 20°C. The final print will look darker under safelighting than the dry test strip did under white light. But resist the temptation to lighten the print by shortening the developing time.

6 WASH AND DRY
Wash the print under running water and dry. Then check to see if it's as good as you hoped. If not you can always adjust the exposure slightly and make another print. The picture above is typical of the quality you should get using the materials, methods and processing described here.

THE CORRECT RESULT
This picture was shot on Ilford FP4 in low sunshine using 1/250 at f8. The print was made on Grade 2 Ilfospeed, slightly light to keep the sunny feel of the shot. Except for the brightest fur on the cat, this picture has good detail, including shaded areas.
The following pictures show some typical errors.

UNDER-EXPOSURE
This was given only half the required exposure during printing – three seconds. Notice the lack of true blacks. Even if the print was developed for twice the normal two minutes it would not look right. Under-development gives a similar result but the whites are greyer and the picture looks flat rather than bright like the one here.

OVER-EXPOSURE
Over-exposure during printing gives a very dark result with no detail in the shadows. This picture had twice the recommended exposure. Again, you cannot correct this mistake by under-developing. A similar effect can happen if you over-develop, but only if you leave the print in the solution for more than normal times.

OUT OF FOCUS
This is an exaggerated example; if you get this, your enlarger's focusing mechanism probably slipped. On a well-focused point you should be able to see the granular structure of a coarse-grained negative clearly enlarged on the paper. If not, your focusing was poor or your lens not a good one.

STAINING
Purple-yellow and other kinds of stain on the print can occur if you forget to use a stop-bath, or if it's exhausted. Similarly, using exhausted fixer causes prints to darken or turn yellow when exposed to light. This also happens when part of a print is not immersed in the fixer. Refix in fresh solution.

UNEVEN DEVELOPMENT
This happens if the print floats to the surface of the developer when you first put it in and you forget to rock the dish or push the print down with the tongs. If you see this happening, immerse the print fully and extend the developing time to three or four minutes to even out the development.

129

Improve your black and white prints

1 ARE YOUR PRINTS SPOTTY?
No matter how hard you clean your negatives, your prints are still likely to have small white marks on them caused by dust, scratches and water deposits. On black and white prints they are most noticeable on featureless grey and black areas. All these marks can be easily and quickly spotted out with retouching medium.

2 SPOTTED INK
Print spotting can be done with either watercolours or dyes. Both are available from art shops. You will need black (white and grey are also useful). Squeeze out a small blob on to a palette or a piece of paper. A good surface to use is the back of a gummed label. The gum gives the ink a glossy finish to match the print.

3 DILUTE THE MEDIUM
You will need a fine 0 or 00 brush made of either sable or squirrel hair. Wet the brush and take a minute amount of the black ink, as small as you can pick up. Work this into a uniform patch of grey, taking up more of the medium. Continue until the grey patch has about the same tone as the area of the print you want to spot.

4 STIPPLE OUT THE SPOT
Hold the brush as shown, with only the very tip touching the print. Dab the loaded brush onto the white areas to build up a stipple of very small grey dots. Keep going until you've covered the whole area. Never use brush strokes, even when filling in lines. Reload the brush as often as it dries.

5 EXAMINE THE PRINT
When you've finished, examine the print in good light. If there is not enough gum in the area the difference in reflectance between the spotted areas (matt) and the rest of the print (gloss) can mean that the spotted areas still show up. Use spray to make the whole print surface a uniform matt or gloss.

6 THE RESULT
The top print is the unspotted original. It was taken with an orange filter to darken the sky and bring out the clouds. This has produced large areas of even grey which show up spots very badly. The print is also badly scratched on the left-hand side. The bottom print shows the same area after spotting.

1 LIGHTENING A PRINT
After processing, this print was seen to be too dark. It had been exposed to bring out detail in the cobbled street, but the dark buildings on the right are also important. Rather than make a new print it is possible to rescue a print like this, which has normal range and contrast but is a shade too dark. The technique is called reduction.

2 MIX THE REDUCER
You will need a chemical called potassium ferricyanide. You can buy it either under a proprietary label or as the chemical itself. Measure out 500ml of water at 20°C and stir in ½ a teaspoon of the crystals until they are dissolved. Note that potassium ferricyanide is a little corrosive and can be poisonous, so take care.

3 SOAK THE PRINT
Arrange three dishes – reducer, water and fixer. First, soak the print in the water bath for one minute so the emulsion is evenly wetted. This will make the action of the reducer more even over the surface of the print. You can use the reducer and the fixer for more than one print, but not the water bath. It must be replaced each time you reduce a print.

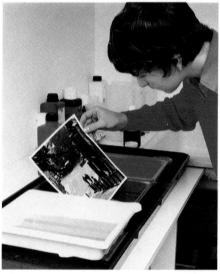

4 INTO THE REDUCER
Immerse the print rapidly and evenly in the reducer. Rock the dish to ensure that all parts of the print are covered. Remove it as soon as the picture approaches the correct tone. Don't wait until the correct tone actually appears as the reducer will continue working after you remove the print.

5 RINSE AND EXAMINE
Quickly immerse the print in the water bath and agitate. The water does not stop the action of the reducer straight away, but it does slow it down. Examine the print. If it is definitely still too dark, put it back into the reducer bath. Otherwise put it into the fixer immediately.

6 FIX, RINSE AND DRY
Give the print one minute in the fixer diluted 1 + 4 at 20°C. Then wash the print thoroughly for 10 minutes. The dried print should not show any sign of yellow staining. In our print, the street cobbles have been reduced to just off white, and there is now much more detail and brightness.

Understanding tones and grades

1 A NORMAL PRINT
This print represents a typical average subject, with a range of tones from black to white and fairly bright contrast. It contains a balance of detail in both the figure and the background, and it's how most people would print this picture. However, it's not the only correct result possible from the negative; it's one of several possibilities.

2 DELIBERATE OVER-EXPOSURE
Making a deliberately dark, heavy print works when there are hidden highlights in the subject, as on the water here. The technique is called over-printing. This print had twice as much exposure as the last one, and the result is very different. Prominence has now been given to the textures in the sand and sea, rather than to the figure.

3 DELIBERATE UNDER-EXPOSURE
Someone else might prefer this result. The subject himself probably would because, unlike the other two prints, it shows his face clearly. The negative was given half the exposure of the first print. The result is totally white sand and little sea detail, but all the tones in the face, clothing and bucket have been revealed this time.

4 ACCIDENTAL UNDER-EXPOSURE
This print cannot be called correctly exposed: it is far too light, and the important textural detail in the old stonework has been lost. However, you can attempt to save it by giving it extra development, using concentrated print developer and a sponge (not a paper towel).

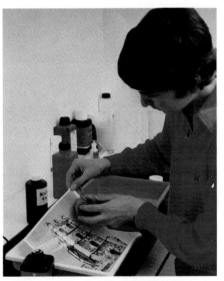

5 BOOSTING DEVELOPMENT
First soak the sponge in hot water and squeeze it out. This is to warm it up. Pour some concentrated print developer onto the sponge and wipe it over the parts of the print you want to darken. Work with the print in the developer bath and keep immersing it to make sure you get an even result.

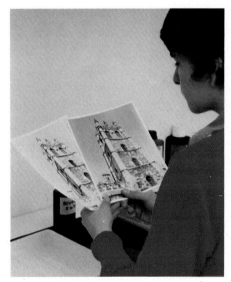

6 THE RESULT
Here you can compare the treated print with an untreated one. You can now see the detail in the stonework and the opportunity has been taken to darken the sky. If you want to boost the whole print rather than just parts of it, simply add some more concentrate to the developer dish and stir it in.

132

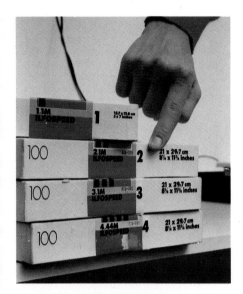

7 GRADES AND CONTRAST
In black and white (but not colour) printing you can buy paper with different degrees of contrast called grades. The number of grades varies with different makes. Ilfospeed paper has four grades: grade 1 (which gives a very soft toned result) up to grade 4 (which gives a crisp, contrasty print with strong blacks and whites).

8 SOFT PAPER
This is the result of printing a negative on grade 1 paper. Notice that the print contains no true blacks; you will only get strong blacks on grade 1 if the negative is very contrasty. Grade 1 is useful for portraits, backlit scenes and over-developed negatives.
Prints made on grade 1 paper may lack impact.

9 NORMAL PAPER
This was printed on average contrast, grade 2 paper. The print does have a full range of tones, but most of them are very close together. You might think this would be the correct paper to print on, having average contrast, but in fact the print still looks soft. The negative needs to be printed on harder paper to bring out the detail.

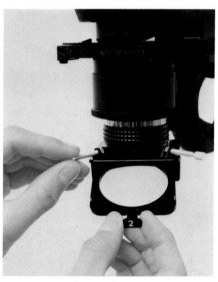

10 HARD PAPER
This was printed on grade 4 paper, and the result is much better. All the fine detail now seems sharper and parts of the picture are picked out in a very strong black. With some negatives the result might just have been a harsh print, but with this one, the picture is given much more impact.

11 ONE PAPER, SEVERAL GRADES
Instead of buying lots of different grades of paper, you can get a multi-contrast printing paper which, when used with special colour filters, will give you all the different grades you'll need. The most widely available paper of this type is Ilford Multigrade which comes with a set of filters.

12 USING THE FILTERS
Ilford market Multigrade filter sets. The colours are yellow and magenta. Yellow is for producing softer grades and magenta for harder. Included in the set is an adjustable filter holder that fits around the enlarger lens barrel. The filters in a colour head will produce the same effect.

133

Selective printing controls

1 SELECTIVE PROCESSING TOOLS
One of the simplest ways of controlling
your prints is to manipulate the light from
the enlarger. You can mask off some of it
to lighten or darken parts of the print
using a piece of card or a special
dodging tool. Or you can produce
unusual-shaped borders, or soften the
picture by holding a diffusion filter
underneath the lens.

2 SIMPLE DODGING AND BURNING
When you stop light reaching part of a
picture, it is called dodging or shading.
Adding extra light to the image is called
burning-in. The method is simple when
the picture has light and dark parts with
a straight division. About halfway
through the exposure, hold some card
over the dark part, moving it slightly to
avoid a hard edge.

3 THE RESULT
The top print is a straightforward
exposure, giving correct tones on the
beach, but the dramatic sky has been
lost through under-exposure. For the
bottom print a further exposure was
given with the card held on the dividing
line between beach and sky to cover the
beach. Now both parts of the picture are
correctly exposed.

4 MORE SELECTIVE BURNING-IN
To dodge and burn more complex
shapes, you can use your hands to
project a spot of light of the right shape
and size. Again, keep moving your hands
to avoid making a sharp patch. You will
need to experiment for a few prints to
find out how much exposure time to
give.

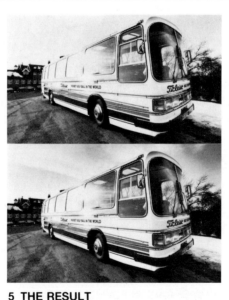

5 THE RESULT
In the top picture the sky has again been
lost through under-exposure, but if you
used a straight piece of card along the
horizon to burn in the sky this time, the
top of the bus would be over-exposed.
Instead, selective hand control was used
to burn in the sky, which was given four
times as much exposure.

6 COMBINED CONTROL
A straight exposure of a shadow falling
across a stone wall produced the top
print. For the lower version, a card was
cut to the right shape and placed almost
in contact with the paper. The shadow
area was then given half the original
exposure and the sunlit area three times
as much.

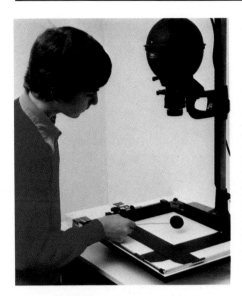

7 THE DODGING TOOL

A disadvantage of using card or your hands is that you can't shade the centre of a print without at the same time shading part of the outside as well. To get round this, cut out a cardboard disc and secure it to some wire. If you carefully keep this moving over the print, the wire won't affect the exposure, but the disc will dodge out the centre.

8 LIGHTENING A FACE

A good use for your dodging tool is to bring out detail in a face. The baby above was photographed in bright sunlight and printed for correct detail in the clothing. Just how much difference can be made is shown in the print below. Here, the face was dodged out to give it just a third of the main exposure. This technique works well with backlit portraits.

9 OVAL PRINTS

You don't need to confine yourself to rectangular prints every time. You can make an oval print, for example, just by masking off part of the paper with an oval cut-out. Keep the mask still and you have a sharp-edged oval; move it about slightly and the image fades away towards the border, an effect known as a vignette.

10 CREATING A VIGNETTE

For this picture an oval mask was held just above the print surface throughout the exposure time and continually moved about to create a soft oval outline. The print itself was kept as light as possible for a high-key effect and to lose background detail. This is a good way to remove a messy background.

11 SOFT FOCUS EFFECTS

If you forget to use a soft focus filter when you took a picture you can produce a similar effect at the printing stage. Simply hold an ordinary soft focus filter beneath your enlarger lens. Cokin and similar system filters work well here. Don't put the filter above the lens or in the enlarger's filter drawer.

12 THE RESULT

Here is the same negative as in step 10, but printed darker and through a soft focus filter. The softening is particularly noticeable on the hair. Soft focus can also hide some of the graininess that may show on larger prints and it can disguise small scratches on the negative.

How to tone prints

The correct term for black and white photography is monochrome because the final result can be a scale of tones in any one colour, not just grey. On normal photographic paper, the tones appear in shades of grey from black to white, but the paper can be treated chemically to give shades of a whole range of colours.

The most familiar toning process is sepia toning, in which shades of grey are replaced by shades of brown to make the print resemble an old photograph. The effect works particularly well with portraits. Another popular colour is blue; it is ideal for seascapes, snow scenes, night-time shots and moonlit effects. These and other colours such as yellow, red, green and mauve, are available in kits.

Toning is usually carried out on a completed black and white print – one that has been developed, fixed and washed.

1 SEPIA TONING: THE KIT
For sepia toning you can use a kit. The one shown here is made by Colorvir. Most kits contain two solutions. One is the bleach bath and is slightly corrosive; the other is the toner solution. Both solutions are in concentrated form and must be diluted before use. You will also need a dish to hold the print, and running water.

2 MAKE UP THE BLEACH
A 20 × 24cm (8 × 10in) print needs about 500ml of liquid to cover it, and the bleach concentrate must be diluted 4:100. So measure out 500ml of water at 20°C and add to it 20ml of bleach concentrate. Mix the solution thoroughly to ensure that it will act evenly.
If your print is dry, have it soaking in water while you do this.

3 BLEACH THE PRINT
Drain the print if it was soaking and place it in the dish. Pour the yellow bleach solution onto the print and rock to keep the bleach moving over the surface of the print. Continue until all the tones, even the darkest blacks, have a brown tinge. This will take at least two to three minutes.

4 TONE THE PRINT
Rinse the print and prepare the toner solution, again using 500ml of water at 20°C and 20ml of concentrate. Pour this onto the print. It will immediately change colour from sandy brown to chocolate, and will then darken fully in about a minute. Store the toner and rinse the print.

5 THE RESULT
You should end up with a print having rich dark browns and whites that are slightly warmer than the original print, but still fairly clean. The exact colour of the print depends on the kit you used, the type of paper, the developer that the original print was processed in and the time of that development.

136

6 BLUE TONING: THE KIT
Blue toners often work as a single solution, where you can immerse the print and watch it change colour. This is the Berg Blue Toner kit from the USA, though others are also available. This kit has two concentrates that have to be mixed together to form the working solution. This solution can be stored for six months.

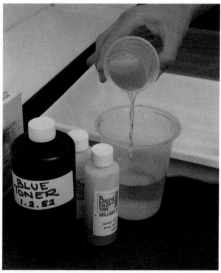

7 MIX THE KIT
Again, you will need about 500ml of solution to cover a 20 × 24cm (8 × 10in) print. Add 100ml of concentrate part A to 250ml of water. Then add 100ml of part B and top up with water to 500ml. (The kit's instructions suggest you make up all of the concentrate at once to form a litre of solution, but you don't have to, as the concentrate will keep longer.)

8 ADD THE TONER
If the print is dry immerse it in water beforehand to make sure that the action of the toner is even – the toner can work extremely quickly. Pour the toner over the print, keeping the stream of toner moving so it's not landing on the same spot for too long. Rock the dish to keep the solution agitated, and be ready to remove the print.

9 JUDGE THE EFFECT
The yellow solution tends to obscure just how blue the print is becoming. This print looks dark blue, but once the solution is washed off it will be much brighter. Don't leave the print in the toner for too long or the highlights will start to turn blue. You can always return the print for more toning later.

10 STORE THE SOLUTION
Do not discard the solution. Pour it into a labelled, dated brown bottle. Berg recommend using a glass bottle rather than a plastic one.
However, a plastic bottle is quite adequate if you plan to use the solution over a period of weeks rather than months.

11 THE RESULT
Wash the print in running water for 10 minutes. Your final print should look like this. The whites have remained fairly clear, though the toner has extended slightly into the highlights. This can only be avoided by giving the print the absolute minimum toning time but it's inevitable if you want a strong blue.

137

Creative effects with sandwich printing

If you are used to printing colour slides or black and white negatives you'll find it just as easy to print a combination of two images instead of just one. This combination is known as a sandwich.

The easiest form of sandwich printing is with two colour slides together. Just by holding the two slides together up to the light you can see immediately what the result will look like. Printing a black and white sandwich is slightly more difficult because you're dealing with negatives. You can't see the final result just by looking at the two images together. And the combined print is not the same as the two individual prints of the images combined together because the tones are reversed on a negative, so take care with your choice of images.

There is, however, a way of combining two individual negatives into one. It's by exposing each one separately onto the same sheet of paper.

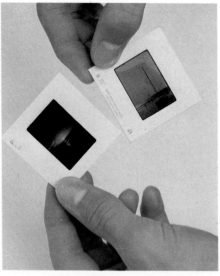

1 COLOUR: SELECT YOUR SLIDES
Go through your slides and find some suitable images to combine. Very simple subjects such as skies, sunsets and seascapes make the best combinations. Complex subjects do not work well; neither do dark subjects – remember that a dark area on one slide will be dark on the combined image. Try to select two slides from the same type of film.

2 THE FIRST IMAGE
This is an ideal foreground image: a strong, simple silhouette against an almost plain background. There is little colour, hardly any shadow, and the sky is completely blank. This picture could be dropped over almost any other image without creating problems. And because it is a very light slide, it does not add much density.

3 THE SECOND IMAGE
This background image will provide almost all the detail in the picture, except where the silhouette of the boat comes through. Make sure your second slide combines well with the first one. Here, the scenes are similar, both are vertical, and they both have the horizon at roughly the same level.

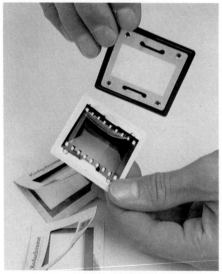

4 COMBINE THE SLIDES
Take the slides out of their present mounts and clean them thoroughly. Clean a glass slide mount in readiness for the slides. Place the slides emulsion side to emulsion side for maximum sharpness. If necessary, stagger the slides to make sure that their horizons match. Now mount them.

5 THE RESULT
Now print the combined slide using reversal printing paper or a print material such as Cibachrome or Agfachrome Speed. Printing exposure will be longer than usual but the silhouette should not affect your standard filtration. The two images should blend together quite naturally.

6 BLACK AND WHITE
This print was selected because it has a plain white sky and a large black area and is ideal to combine, either by sandwiching, where the detail will appear in the cloak, or by double exposure, where the detail will appear in the sky. The film doesn't need to be of the same type here, so long as the negative densities are similar.

7 THE SECONDARY NEGATIVE
This will be the secondary negative, chosen because it does not have a strong subject. Instead, it shows an abstract pattern of surf and is almost evenly grey all over. It does not stand on its own as a picture but will work well combined with another. If you don't have a suitable secondary image you could shoot one specially.

8 COMBINE THE NEGATIVES
Place the two strips of negatives next to each other, again emulsion side to emulsion side for sharpness. Get their relative positions roughly right, then put them into your negative carrier. Place the carrier in the enlarger and switch it on so you can see the combined image. Now get the images in exactly the right position.

9 THE RESULT
With a negative sandwich details appearing as dark areas on one negative can only print if they coincide with clear or thin areas on the other negative. This means that in our example the sea won't print over the sky because this is black on the negative. It will only print on the pale areas.

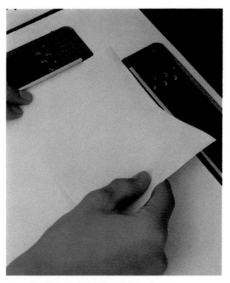

10 DOUBLE EXPOSURE
An alternative way of combining two black and white prints is by double exposure. Use a paper easel like this so you can position the paper accurately. Expose the first negative. Then remove the paper while you replace it with the second negative. Return the paper to the easel and expose again.

11 THE RESULT
Double exposure has produced a more effective result in this case because the surf has printed over the plain sky but less so over the girl. The picture now conveys the image much better. Each picture was given half the exposure normally needed to produce a correct density print.

Making extra large prints

If a photograph looks good when it's at the enprint size the chances are it'll look even better when it's blown up large. Medium-speed 35mm films can be enlarged to as much as 50×60cm (20×24in) and still give fairly acceptable quality.

Not all enlargers are suitable for making extra-large prints. You have to be able to move the enlarger's head or column to project an image of the right size; the lamp must be powerful enough for you to see the image clearly and the enlarger must have a good quality lens.

For black and white work you will need two dishes large enough to take the large-size paper. If your darkroom is small, then you can use only one processing dish.

For extra-large colour prints the method is much the same as for small prints, except that you will need a large drum – the processing dishes are too inconvenient to be used successfully.

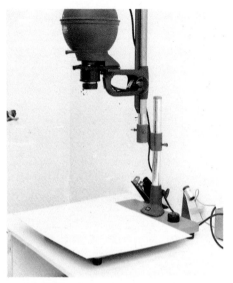

1 EXTENDING YOUR ENLARGER
The first step is to project a large enough image. One way is to extend the enlarger column so you can move the head further away from the baseboard. If the column is 30mm (1¼in) thick then you can buy an extension like the one shown above. It also moves the negative further out so you can use wider paper. Some enlargers have special extensions.

2 PROJECTING ON TO THE FLOOR
Another way is to turn the head or column round and move the enlarger to the edge of the bench so it projects on to the floor. Make sure you place a heavy weight on the baseboard to balance the enlarger. Check that the floor and the enlarger head are parallel; if they aren't, you won't be able to focus the entire image at once.

3 LARGE PRINT EASELS
For large paper sizes you don't need to buy an expensive masking easel. Use a large piece of card, as in picture 1, or buy a simple large paper easel, as above. This easel is black to minimize reflections and increase contrast. It produces borderless prints size 30×40cm (12×16in) or less.

4 FOCUSING AT FLOOR LEVEL
You can use a special large focus finder, such as the Unicolor one shown here. This allows you to see the focused image and adjust the focusing control on the enlarger at the same time. Ordinary focus finders are less suitable because you have to keep getting down to see the image.

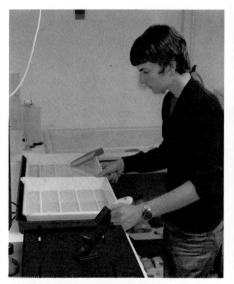

5 TWO-DISH PROCESSING
To process prints up to 40×50cm (16×20in) you need use only two dishes instead of three. The first dish contains developer and the second water and fixer alternately. You place the developed print in the second dish, rinse it, discard the water then add the fixer. Rebottle the fixer afterwards.

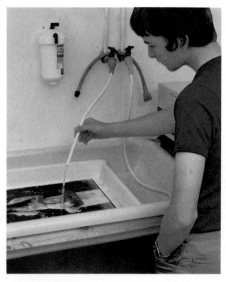

6 SINGLE-DISH PROCESSING
For larger prints such as 50 × 60cm
(20 × 24in) it's often convenient to use
just one dish for the processing,
especially if your darkroom is small.
Place the print in the dish, emulsion side
facing up, and pour your developer over
it. Keep moving your hand as you pour to
cover the whole print surface and
prevent a hot-spot from forming.

7 DEVELOPING AND FIXING
Use a slow-working developer with
dilution adjusted so that development
will take about two minutes or longer.
Then you need use only a small amount
(1000ml). Rock this over the image until it
is evenly developed. Return developer to
its container, rinse, then add 1000ml of
fixer diluted 1 + 3. Rock this over the
print for two-three minutes.

8 WASHING
Big prints need careful washing. Use a
short hose to direct water over the print.
Wash each quarter individually for five
minutes. With RC paper, do this
emulsion side upwards – it's the
emulsion that absorbs the chemicals,
not the base. Keep the print covered
while washing and use a fast flow of
water.

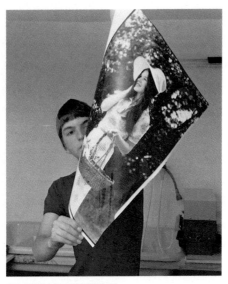

9 WIPE THE PRINT
A large print carries a lot more surface
water than a small one, so it helps to
remove as much water as you can before
you leave it to dry. If you are quick and
do not let the emulsion become tacky,
you can wipe the print with kitchen paper
towel to remove excess moisture. This
will also improve surface sheen.

10 DRY THE PRINT
The print will probably be too large for
you to dry hanging it in a drying cabinet.
If so, attach a clip to one of the corners –
keeping it away from the image area –
and hang it up to dry in a well-ventilated
room. An RC paper should take about 30
minutes. When it's dry, trim off any spare
paper.

11 EXTRA-LARGE COLOUR PRINTS
The technique for making large colour
prints is much the same as for small
ones, though prints larger than
40 × 60cm (16 × 24in) are expensive
and difficult to process. You cannot
afford failures. Here, a 30 × 40cm
(12 × 16in) drum is being loaded – make
sure you bend the paper the right way.

Glossary

A

Angle of view This is the maximum angle seen by a lens. Most so-called standard or normal lenses (for example 50mm on a 35mm camera) have an angle of view of about 50°. Lenses of long focal length (200mm for example) have narrower angles and lenses of short focal length (eg 28mm) have wider angles of view.

Autowinder In the strictest sense an autowinder is a unit which can be attached to many SLRs for motorized single frame film advance. After each exposure the autowinder automatically advances the film to the next frame and cocks the shutter. Many units, however, are capable of modest speed picture sequences. Some cameras have an autowinder built into the main body.

B

B camera setting A shutter set to B remains open while the shutter release is depressed.

Bellows A concertina-like unit that fits between the camera body and the lens. A bellows unit enables the lens to focus on close subjects, and gives a large image of the subject. The magnification of the subject depends on the focal length of the lens and the extension of the bellows. For example, using a bellows unit with a 50mm lens on a 35mm camera gives a subject magnification range of about x1 (that is, life-size) to x3.

Burning-in A printing technique where extra exposure is selectively given to parts of the image. In black and white printing burning-in darkens tones and modifies contrast (when using multicontrast papers); it is particularly useful for bringing out highlights. In colour printing, burning-in can modify both tone (density) and colour.

C

Cable release A flexible cable which is attached (usually screwed in) to the shutter release and used for relatively long exposure times (⅛ to several seconds). The operator depresses the plunger on the cable to release the shutter remotely. This prevents the camera from moving during the exposure.

Cadmium sulphide cell (CdS) A type of cell used in some hand-held light meters and some built-in camera meters. The resistance of the cell to a constant electrical voltage (supplied by a battery) changes as the light falling on the cell varies. The resulting current is either used to move a pointer on a scale or employed directly to alter the camera's shutter speed or aperture. CdS cells are more sensitive than selenium cells and are ideal when photographing in dim lighting conditions.

CC filters These are 'colour correcting' or 'colour compensating' filters which may be used either in front of the camera or when printing colour film to modify the final overall colour of the photograph. Their various strengths are indicated by numbers usually ranging from 05 to 50. Filters may be combined to give a complete range of colour correction.

Close-up attachment Any attachment which enables the camera to focus closer than its normal closest distance. Such attachments include close-up lenses, bellows and extension tubes.

Colour balance The overall colour cast of the film or print. Normally a film or print is balanced to give grey neutrals (such as a road or pavement) and pleasing skin tones. The colour balance preferred by the viewer is a subjective choice, and this is the reason for the variety of colour films available, each having its own colour characteristics.

Complementary colours These are pairs of colours which, when mixed together, give a grey (neutral). For example, a grey is formed when yellow and blue light are mixed together, therefore, yellow is complementary to blue and vice versa. Other complementary colours include green and magenta, red and cyan.

Contact printing In this type of printing the film is held in contact with the printing paper and no lens is needed. Contact printing can be used for making prints from large films or when contacts are required for inspection or records.

Continuous tone Any photographic material which is capable of producing a continuous range of tones from white to a maximum black. A continuous tone material shows subtlety of tone throughout its range, from rich shadows, through mid-greys, to delicate highlights.

Conversion filter Any filter which converts one standard light source to another standard light source. For example, a Wratten 85B filter converts daylight to photoflood-type illumination. The filter, when placed in front of the camera lens, enables a camera loaded with tungsten colour film to give correct colour photographs in daylight. To compensate for the light absorbed by the filter, it is necessary to give extra exposure. This is determined by the filter factor.

D

Depth of field The distance between the nearest and furthest points of the subject which are acceptably sharp. Depth of field can be increased by using small apertures (large f numbers), and/or short focal-length lenses and/or by taking the photograph from further away. Use of large apertures (small f numbers), long focal-length lenses, and near subjects reduces depth of field.

Depth of field preview A facility available on many SLR cameras which stops down the lens to the shooting aperture so that the depth of field can be seen.

Differential focusing The technique of using wide apertures (small f numbers) to reduce depth of field, and to therefore separate the focused subject from its foreground and background.

Diffused image An image which has indistinct edges and appears 'soft'. Overall- or partially-diffused images can be produced in the camera by using special lenses and filters, or by shooting through various 'filmy' substances such as vaseline, sellotape, and fine stockings. Images may also be diffused during enlarging by placing a diffusing device between the enlarging lens and the paper.

Diffuse light source Any light source which produces indistinct and relatively light shadows with soft outline. The larger and more even the light source is the more diffuse will be the resulting illumination. Any light source bounced into a large reflecting surface (for example, a white umbrella, white card, or large dish reflector) will produce diffuse illumination.

Diopter A measurement unit which is used to indicate the power of a lens. The diopter power is the reciprocal of the lens focal length, ie 1/F in metres. For example, a lens of 1m focal length is a 1 diopter lens, a 500mm lens is 2 diopters, a 250mm lens is 4 diopters. Most close-up lenses have their strength expressed in diopters and when two or more lenses are used together their combined strength is found by adding the diopter values.

Dodging The technique used during enlarging which reduces exposure in certain parts of the image by blocking the light. A dodging tool is moved gently above those areas of the picture which require lightening (or darkening if printing from a transparency) while the remainder of the image receives the full exposure.

E

Easel Also known as an enlarging easel or a masking frame. It holds the photographic paper flat while an enlarged image is projected on to it. The easel also controls the size and squareness of the print borders.

Emulsion A photographic emulsion is the light-sensitive layer (or layers) which is coated on to the film or paper base. It consists of silver halide salts suspended in gelatin.

Exposure The result of allowing light to act on a photosensitive material.

The amount of exposure depends on both the intensity of light and the time it is allowed to fall on the sensitive material.

Exposure latitude The maximum variation of film or paper exposure from the 'correct' exposure which still yields acceptable results. For example, most colour negative films have an exposure latitude of −1 (one stop under) to +2 (two stops over). Exposure latitude depends on the actual film in use, processing, the subject and its lighting, and what is considered as acceptable to the photographer.

Exposure meter An instrument which measures the intensity of light falling on (incident reading) or reflected by (reflected reading) the subject. Exposure meters can be separate or built into a camera; the latter type usually gives a readout in the viewfinder and may also automatically adjust the camera settings to give correct exposure.

Extension rings (tubes) Spacer rings which fit between the camera body and the lens, and allow the camera to focus on subjects closer than the nearest marked focusing distance of the lens. A set of rings typically allows a focusing range of 56-20cm for a standard 50mm lens. These extension rings may be non-automatic or automatic; the latter type allow full-aperture focusing just prior to exposure.

F

Fast films Films that are very sensitive to light and require only a small exposure. They are ideal for photography in dimly lit places, or where fast shutter speeds (for example, 1/500) and/or small apertures (for example f16) are desired. These fast films (400 ISO or more) are more grainy than slower films.

Filter Any material which, when placed in front of a light source or lens, absorbs some of the light coming through it. Filters are usually made of glass, plastic, or gelatin-coated plastic and in photography are mainly used to modify the light reaching the film, or in colour printing to change the colour of the light reaching the paper.

Flare A term used to describe stray light that is not from the subject and which reaches the film. Flare has the overall effect of lowering image contrast and is most noticeable in the subject shadow areas. It is eliminated or reduced by using coated lenses (most modern lenses are multi-coated), lens hoods and by preventing lights from shining directly into the lens.

f numbers The series of internationally agreed numbers which are marked on lenses and indicate the brightness of the image on the film plane – so all lenses are focused on infinity. The f number series is 1·4, 2, 2·8, 4, 5·6, 8, 11, 16, 22, 32 etc – changing to the next largest number (for example, f11 to f16) decreases the image brightness to ½, and moving to the next smallest number doubles the image brightness.

Focal length The distance between the optical centre of the lens (not necessarily within the lens itself) and the film when the lens is focused on infinity. Focal length is related to the angle of view of the lens – wide angle lenses have short focal lengths (for example 28mm) and narrow angle lenses have long focal lengths (for example, 200mm).

Full-aperture metering Any through-the-lens (TTL) light metering system that operates with the lens at maximum aperture.

G

Graininess The subjective measurement of the grain pattern. For instance, fast films when greatly enlarged produce images that are very grainy, and slow films give relatively 'grainless' images.

I

ISO International Standards Organization. The ISO number indicates the film speed and aims to replace the dual ASA and DIN systems. For example, a film rating of ASA 100, 21 DIN becomes ISO 100/21˚.

L

Leaf shutter A type of lens shutter which is usually built into a lens and operates by several metal blades opening outwards to reveal the diaphragm aperture and then closing when the exposure time is completed. Leaf shutters have the advantage of being able to synchronize with flash at any speed but have a top speed of only 1/500 second.

LEDs Light emitting diodes. These are electronic devices for displaying information. They are used for a number of photographic purposes, including the indication of under- or over-exposure, or the selected aperture/shutter speed combination. LEDs are usually visible in the camera viewfinder.

Long focus lens Commonly used slang for 'long focal length lens', which means any lens with a greater focal length than a standard lens, for example, 85mm, 135mm and 300mm lenses on a 35mm camera. These long focal length lenses are ideal for portraiture, sports and animal photography.

M

Mirror lens Any lens which incorporates mirrors instead of conventional glass (or plastic) lens elements. This type of lens design is employed mainly for long focal length lenses (eg 500mm), and produces a relatively lightweight lens with a fixed aperture (about f8).

Monochrome A monochrome picture is one which has only one colour; the term is usually applied to black and white prints or slides.

Motor-drive A motor-drive provides motorized film advance, both single frame and sequence. Motor-drive units are generally capable of much faster sequence rates (given in frames per second – fps) than auto-winders and can be used with a wider range of accessories.

Multiple exposure The process of making more than one exposure on the same piece of film, thus allowing one image to be built on top of another. Multiple exposure is easy to achieve with large studio and most medium-format cameras, but can be difficult with smaller cameras (35mm, 110 etc) because most have a double exposure prevention system whereby the film must be advanced to tension the shutter.

O

Open up A slang term which means to use a larger aperture (for example, from f8 to f5·6). The opposite term is 'close down', that is reduce the aperture.

P

Panning The act of swinging the camera to follow a moving object to keep the subject's position in the viewfinder approximately the same. The shutter is released during the panning movement.

R

Reciprocity law failure Failure of the reciprocity law (which states: exposure = image brightness at the focal plane × shutter speed) manifests itself in loss of sensitivity of the film emulsion and occurs when exposure times are either long or very short. The point of departure from the law depends on the particular film but for most camera films it occurs outside the range ½-1/1000 second, when extra exposure is needed.

Red eye This 'bloodshot' appearance of eyes can occur when taking portraits with a flashgun attached to the camera. It is avoided by moving the flashgun away from the camera.

Reversal material Any film or paper which gives a positive directly from a positive (for example, slide film or Cibachrome paper), or a negative directly from a negative.

S

Safelight A coloured light which does not fog the photographic material being used. For example, a yellow-orange safelight does not emit blue light, and is therefore suitable when working with materials sensitive only to blue light.

Saturation The purity of a colour. The purest colours are spectrum colours (100% saturation) and the least pure are greys (0% saturation).

Slave unit A light-sensitive device which triggers other flash sources when activated by the light from the camera-connected flash. The use of slave units does away with the need for trailing leads and also allows for more remote placing of the flashguns.

Spot meter An exposure meter which reads off a very small area of the subject. Spot meters have an acceptance angle of only one or two degrees. Their usefulness depends on careful interpretation by the photographer.

Standard lens The lens most often used, and considered by most photographers and camera manufacturers to be the one which gives an image most closely resembling normal eye vision. The normal lens for 35mm cameras has a focal length of around 50mm.

Stop Another term for aperture or exposure control. For example, to reduce exposure by two stops means to either reduce the aperture (f8 to f16) or increase the shutter speed (1/60 sec to 1/250 sec) by two settings. To 'stop down' a lens is to reduce the aperture, that is, increase the f number.

Stopping down The act of reducing the lens aperture size ie, increasing the f number. Stopping down increases the depth of field and is often used in landscape and advertising work, where sharp detail is needed over all the subject.

T

Teleconverter An optical device which is placed between the camera body and lens, and increases the magnification of the image. For example, a ×2 converter when combined with a 50mm lens, gives effectively a 100mm lens.

Telephoto lens A long focal-length lens of special design to minimize its physical lrength. Most narrow angle lenses are of telephoto design.

W

Wide angle lens A short focal-length lens which records a wide angle of view. It is used for landscape studies and when working in confined spaces.

Z

Zoom lens Alternative name for a lens having a range of focal lengths. One zoom lens can replace several fixed focal-length lenses, but results are likely to be inferior.

Index

PHOTOGRAPHIC CREDITS

Cover photograph Ray Daffurn – All photographs in this book by David Kilpatrick/Eaglemoss; apart from: 6-7 Michael Busselle/Eaglemoss – 8 (centre) John Goldblatt, (right) Tina Rogers – 9 (centre top) Steve Bicknell/Eaglemoss, (top left, top right) Jack Schofield – 10 Malkolm Warrington/Eaglemoss – 12 (left) Alfred Gregory, (right) Tom Nebbia/Aspect – 13 (top) Ed Buziak – 14 Malcolm Aird/Eaglemoss – 15 (bottom right) Tim Beddow, (top) Steve Bicknell/Eaglemoss – 17 (bottom right) Robert Ashby – 23 (centre bottom) Tim Beddow – 24 (bottom right) Anne Conway, 25 (bottom left) Steve Lister – 29 (bottom right) Steve Lister – 33 (top left) Steve Bicknell/Eaglemoss, (bottom) T A Lovell – 38 (bottom right) Eric Crichton/Courtesy of Worldwide Butterfly Farm – 46 (top) John Garrett, (bottom) Neill Meneer – 47 (bottom) Jack Schofield – 48 (bottom right) Jack Schofield – 49 (bottom left) James Harrison – 51 (top right) Lawrence Lawry/Eaglemoss – 53 (top) Michael Busselle/Eaglemoss – 56 (centre bottom) Anne Conway, (bottom right) Lawrence Lawry/Eaglemoss – 70 (top) John Garrett – 74 (bottom left) Richard Steedman/Image Bank – 75 (bottom left) Jack Schofield, (top right) John Benton Harris – 76 (bottom left) Shirley Kilpatrick – 79 (bottom left) Rémy Poinot – 84 (bottom right) England Scene Picture Library – 91 (top) David Parker – 93 (bottom left) A Houghton – 94 (left) Al Coburn/George Eastman House, (right) Anne Conway. All illustrations by Clive Spong/Linden Artists; apart from: 8-11 Rich Designs – 12-13 Christian Baker Associates – 14 (top) Rich Designs, (bottom) Jim Bamber – 15 Jim Bamber – 16 Drury Lane Studios – 18-19 David Parker – 20-22 Drury Lane Studios – 26-27 Rich Designs – 30-31 Rich Designs – 32 Jenny Pentecost – 34-36 Rich Designs – 38 Rich Designs – 41 Jenny Pentecost – 44 Rich Designs – 46-49 Rich Designs – 51-53 Jenny Pentecost – 74-75 Jenny Pentecost – 78 Jenny Pentecost – 82 Jenny Pentecost – Endpapers Colin Molyneux.